AF512271

Security in a Complex Era:
Emerging Challenges Facing India

Security in a Complex Era: Emerging Challenges Facing India

Neil Padukone

Observer Research Foundation
New Delhi

KNOWLEDGE WORLD

KW Publishers Pvt Ltd
New Delhi

KNOWLEDGE WORLD
KW Publishers Pvt Ltd
NEW DELHI: 4676/21, First Floor, Ansari Road, Daryaganj, New Delhi 110002
E mail@kwpub.in/knowledgeworld@vsnl.net T +91.11.23263498 / 43528107
MUMBAI: 15 Jay Kay Industrial Estate, Linking Road Extn., Santacruz (W), Mumbai 400054
E mumbai@kwpub.in T +91.22.26614110 / 26613505

www.kwpub.in

All rights reserved. No part of this book may be reproduced or transmitted in any form or by any means, electronic or mechanical, including photocopying, recording or by any information storage and retrieval system, without permission in writing.

ISBN 13: 978-93-80502-12-0

Copyright © 2010, Observer Research Foundation, New Delhi

Published by Kalpana Shukla, KW Publishers Pvt Ltd
4676/21, First Floor, Ansari Road, Daryaganj, New Delhi 110002

Printed and Bound in India

Contents

Foreword by General V.P. Malik (Retd) ix

Executive Summary xi

Introduction xxv

Micro Level Challenges 1

The Information Revolution and the Role of Perception 1

Identity 2

Perception Management and Perception Influence 5

Networked Organisation 6

Networked Threats 7

Communication in Networks 9

Information and Communications Technologies 11

Religious Extremist, Ideological and Nationalist Groups 14

Economic Networks 19

Narcotics Trafficking 20

Arms Proliferation 21

Human Trafficking 22

Organised Crime Syndicates 23

The Trans-national Dimensions 24

Nexus 26

The Threat of Governance 27

Personnel Retention and Morale 27

Privatisation and Accountability 27

Systemic Enablers of Corruption and Mismanagement 29

Expectations and Realities of a 'Flailing' State 31

Macro Level Challenges 33
Perception at the Macro Level 34
Perception Management in the State System 35
State Perceptions: Pakistan 36
State Perceptions: China 41
State Perceptions: India's Smaller Neighbours 43
State-to-State Conflict 43
International Engagements in a New Global Order 44
The Indian Ocean 45
Further Afield 49
Nuclear Policy 50
Utility of Nuclear Weapons in an Age of Complexity 50
Nuclear 'Strategy' 53
Space Policy 56
Civilian Development vs. Militarisation vs. Weaponisation 56
Civilian Capacities 58
Technology and Information in Military Affairs 59
Emerging India and Strategic Culture 61

Micro-Macro Interactions 65
Nuclear Security 65
Frontier Security 67
Political Issues 67
Logistical Issues 69
Technological Drivers of Conflict 70
Cyber Warfare 70
Information and Its Security 72
Emerging Technologies 73
The Environment, Climate Change and National Security 76
Rising Temperature 78
Extremes and Anomalies in Weather 78
Rising Sea Levels 79
Himalayan Glaciers 79
Resource Wars 80

Governance of the Environment 82
Poverty and Economics in the Realm of Security 87
Economics as Instruments of State Policy 87
Conflict Economies 88
The Military-Industrial Complex 89
Urbanisation, Migration and Development 91
Poverty and Economic Stratification 93
The Nation and the State in the 21st Century: Perceptions at the Micro-Macro Level 95

Conclusion: Managing Security in a Complex Age 101
A Complex Era 101
An Evolutionary Systems View of National Security 104
A Systems View 104
Evolutionary Perspectives: Stability and Change 105
Foresight and Action 107
Anticipatory Governance 107
Diverse Thinking 108
Networked Management 109
Conclusion 113

Notes 115

Foreword

India is a bigger economic and political power today than it has been at any time since its independence. Yet, the intellectual tools and mechanisms that shape its world view, foreign and security policies and its sense of strategy remain rooted in another era. Security environment analysis and related policy advocacy is the domain of a small club of retired diplomats and generals in Delhi, with a few journalists thrown in. The result: far and few changes in our policies despite unprecedented dynamics of global, regional and domestic security factors. Captain B.H. Liddel-Hart has rightly said: "The only thing harder than getting a new idea in is to get an old one out!"

When Neil Padukone wrote to me that he wanted to do a project on *The Future of Conflict and Security in India's Emerging Political Environment* with the Observer Research Foundation, I felt it was a good opportunity to get an outsider's view—of an American of Indian descent. Neil's scholarly and proven academic credentials, I had hoped, would give a different look at the subject. That hope has, indeed, been realised.

Most Indians, when asked about India's security threats and challenges, would say, "These are our external threats, these are our internal threats and, today, they are a little meshed." But there is a lot that is happening in the world, the Southern Asian region, and, most importantly, within India itself, that we miss when scrutinising the developing security and conflict situation. Neil's look at India's strategic environment focusses on the happenings and the new milieu. In doing so, he anticipates some emerging trends.

He has studied the subject in three major segments, focussing more on the scale of organisation rather than political borders — which, as we have seen in recent years, can provide a false sense of infallibility. The analysis looks at:

- The realm of individuals and groups, i.e. the micro level challenges.
- The realm of nation-states and global systems, i.e. the macro level challenges.
- The meeting ground between the above two.

Many of us do not realise how fast India itself is changing. Our value systems are changing and our economic and social systems are under flux. We are united when there is a crisis. But otherwise, we are very nearly at war with each other on very small issues. The very same information and networking technologies that have enabled us to work together and grow economically have also brought us into conflict with one another. Their full positive and negative impact is yet to be comprehended. We can observe the challenges of what is happening around us—the caste, tribal, linguistic and religion-based socio-political divides, political polarisation, mob mentality (mobocracy), terrorism encouraged by Naxalism and fundamentalism, and so on. But, as a society that is diverse and deep-rooted in centuries-old history, culture, and thinking, how do we change our approach to such analysis and challenges?

The monograph focuses on the conceptual shifts in the nature of conflict. They include: security threats posed by the networked forms of organisation; the heightened role of information and perceptions in shaping and resolving conflicts; deficits in governance as a security threat; security implications of emerging technologies, climate change and economics; emerging challenges in nuclear, space, and military strategies, and, finally; the global shifts in geopolitical power and their effects on India's strategic scene. The monograph concludes by proposing a new paradigm for conceptualising and acting on national security: an evolutionary systems view of security that employs networked management and anticipatory governance.

Most of this work is based on a concept of complexity theory, which is based neither on ideology nor on the theories of realism and liberalism. This one looks at how relationships between parts give rise to the collective behaviours of a system and how systems interact. The result is quite an 'out of the box' perspective, and suggests a shift in the way we should look and act upon security related issues in India.

V. P. Malik June 2009
General (Retired)
President, ORF Institute of Security Studies,
New Delhi

Executive Summary

Introduction

The world has undergone shifts in economic and political power due in part to new technologies. The instruments of power—financial, governance, communications, military might, etc.—are no longer under the exclusive control of the state, and the very concept of *sovereignty* has been redefined.

The new era has broadened the potential base of security challenges to diverse sources—economic, environmental, social, technological, among others. The highly *networked* nature of threats has brought about a situation where the systems of challenges that India faces are inherently *non-linear*. That is, a minor event in one part of a system may have huge consequences for the whole, while a major event in the system may have a disproportionately small effect.

These non-linear changes occur simultaneously on different scales: on the *micro* level, that of individuals and groups; the *macro* level, at the nation-states and global systems level; and *micro-macro interactions*, the nexus between these two.

Micro Level Challenges

The information and technological revolution of the 1990s has revolutionised the way people are able to communicate and organise themselves. Individuals and groups are able to exert greater pressures on sub-national, national, and even international systems.

The Information Revolution and the Role of Perception

The transmission of information has become the backbone of a new social order immensely heightening the role of *perceptions,* the aggregation of inter-subjectively processed and contextualised information.

Security itself can be understood as *perceived* confidence in the current or future state of affairs. The occurrence of a *security dilemma*, most often cited with regards to international politics, also occurs on the micro scale between individuals and groups.

The credibility of traditional sources of power (particularly the state) has ebbed. In its wake, new sources of authority and allegiance have emerged, and the role played by alternative *identities*—the ways in which collective affiliation is perceived, defined and acted upon—in social and political affairs has increased.

New media outlets and decentralisation of perception control mode makes the realm of perception far more complex. Mobile phones, news media, websites, and social networks contribute to the diffusion and management of perceptions.

Networked Organisation

Both a cause and effect of the empowerment of individuals and groups are *networks,* which are decentralised and distributed forms of social organisation comprising links between nodes (the agents in a network).

A network may extend in all directions, making it difficult to pinpoint its start and end. The organisational structures of networks are capable of change and *adaptation* in the face of impediments. In turn, a key advantage that networks have over hierarchical communication systems is that they are highly distributed, decentralised and more resilient.

Analysing networks enables an understanding of important relationships, the key areas of influence within an organisation, and what gives organisations their strength. Understanding the informal power structures of a system can enable an observer to use the existing dynamics to influence the system as a whole. Ultimately, however, the primary mode of influence in a network is the common narrative—the shared, institutionalised perception that unites the agents in a network.

Religious Extremist, Ideological and Nationalist Groups

The existence and rise of hostile and violent *identity* networks will colour the spectrum of conflict in India for years to come. These identity networks take three major forms that are not necessarily mutually exclusive: insurgency, terrorism, and communalism.

The enhanced complexity of strategic space—due to redundancy, adaptability and perception management in networks—enhances the threat posed by identity networks. A group's ability to learn and adapt is a primary determinant of the level of threat it poses.

Economic Networks

Economic transfer networks shape security challenges by (1) directly financing adversaries and their criminal activities; (2) detracting finances from legitimate concerns; (3) breaching the law and harming people directly; and (4) representing nefarious issues that are more intrinsic to governance;

Such economic networks include *hawala*, unregulated banking, narcotics trafficking, arms proliferation and human trafficking. Organised crime provides the glue that binds pernicious and even licit networks at several levels and can extend its geographic and industry-based influence into the future.

Diasporas, global markets and foreign governments play a central role in these nefarious networks in India. However, while many internal threats are supported and bolstered by outside sources, more often than not, the initial impetus is given by *domestic*, internal issues, which are only later exploited by external forces. Therefore, the internal space of opportunity for manipulation and the environment that enables such manipulation must be minimised, if not eliminated.

The Threat of Governance

The opening of markets has made military and government recruitment economically less attractive than their private sector equivalents and long-term prospects for sustaining government enrolment stands affected.

In the past decades, outsourcing and privatisation of government services has risen in order to increase efficiency. But this bring with it questions of accountability and control over the use of force.

Systemic enablers of corruption and mismanagement in the Indian governance system can precipitate massive security breaches, opening the way for further threats in the future. Lack of faith in the Indian governance system may impel movement towards potentially nefarious sources of authority. Corruption in government services can have the effect of abetting criminals and other nefarious elements. Likewise, governance will experience major systemic challenges if its bureaucratic structure does not match the level of complexity of the environment it faces.

India has been aptly described as a "*flailing* state," in which the head (policies, plans, laws, commissions, government apparatuses, etc) works satisfactorily, but the body and limbs (institutions, governance, bureaucracy, work culture, and *process* of implementing the mandates of the head) are either paralysed or flailing.

The most prominent security implication of this disjointedness in governance is on policy-making and execution. If policies made to address a threat are improperly executed due to weak governance *processes*, the threat remains unaddressed.

When governance itself—the response mechanism to threats—is unable to function effectively, any issue can become a threat.

Macro Level Challenges

India's role in the international system will likely be defined by a few key structural developments: the empowerment of non-state actors, new technologies, and India's anticipated role as a rising power.

How India engages with the world is fundamentally up to India alone. Standing on the verge of great power status, India must take advantage of, and *create,* opportunities while dealing with a great deal of challenges that will no longer come from point-sources.

Perception at the Macro Level

Security at the inter-state level is largely a result of *perceptions*. Deterrence, raising the perceived costs of an action in order to prevent its execution is a tool of perception management. At the state-to-state level, security itself can be understood as incongruence between a threat posed (the *perceived* intentions and projected capabilities of an adversary) and the ability to deal with the threat (one's own capabilities).

In the case of Indo-Pakistani relations, long seen within South Asia and without as the key international issue of the region, perceived enmity stems in part from various understandings of the two states' foundational ethos. As a result of a void in domestic identity and a perceived perennial external threat (and a domestic system that reinforces military rule and militarism) Pakistan has made congenital antipathy to India the core substance of its identity, and its own goals focused against India's success, rather than seeking a viable status of its own.

India fuels this antipathy by responding with similar animosity. Pakistan is generally thought to be the single source of every threat. This excessive focus on Pakistani malevolence turns around on India, as it ostensibly validates Pakistan's fears of a hostile India—resulting in a vicious circle of suspicion. It allows India to ignore the internal problems that *enable* many threats to materialise and also constrains it from expanding its own international engagement.

This problem will remain insurmountable unless (a) Pakistan undergoes a domestic revolution in which its own identity and development are defined in ways that do not necessitate opposition to India; or (b) India seeks to alter the scale and ambit of the relationship, by redefining its own vision of itself in the world and looking beyond South Asia as its only sphere of influence.

China has increasingly begun to cultivate strong relations with India's immediate neighbours, developing a "String of Pearls" strategy, ostensibly to encircle India. However, whether China's "String of Pearls" should be perceived as a *security threat* is up to India alone. If China's capacity and intent are thought to be hostile, then India needs to create its own response capabilities to diminish the magnitude of the perceived Chinese threat.

The fear of India's smaller neighbours, perceived or otherwise, of hegemonistic dominance, makes them retreat from even positive engagements with their larger neighbour. India needs to create a balance between its global power projection and its regional aspirations.

In many ways, inter-linkages (economic, decentralised political ties, and others), power asymmetry, political backlash and fear of escalation serve as deterrents to all-out conventional war in the modern age. Asymmetries in power between India and its smaller neighbours have largely deterred or rendered conventional war unlikely. For this reason, India's adversaries have been forced to rely on asymmetric conflict such as proxy conflict, support for insurgencies and far more decentralised modes of confrontation to counter the notion of domination by India.

International Engagements in a New Global Order

The past ten or fifteen years have witnessed the extension of the active area of Indian foreign policy well beyond the South Asian and regional borders. Increased economic ties have precipitated political engagements, and this trend is likely to continue.

The Indian Ocean has since ancient times been the nation's field of activity, providing economic benefits, influence, security, and also certain vulnerabilities. On the one hand, the ocean has been an open field for mercantile trade and now provides access to the world's emerging energy markets and, on the other, it creates issues vis-à-vis the protection of Indian interests abroad, as well as new forms of maritime conflict.

Recently, India has begun to invest in energy and infrastructure projects in places as diverse as Africa, Latin America, Central Asia, the Middle East and even Russia. Threats to these investments come from local sources as well as in transit (i.e. Indian investments bear the brunt of political issues and weak governance in the countries of investment). If India becomes an increasingly strong political and military player in the world, its role in *international military coalitions* would become more pronounced, resulting in the commitment of troops to regions with varying terrains and battlefield requirements which, in turn, would bring about issues such as armed forces' interoperability and common defence planning.

Nuclear Policy

Nuclear deterrence—the *raison d'etre* of most nuclear strategy—has been based on the concept of *Mutually Assured Destruction* (MAD). But this concept is not foolproof. Today, nuclear threats may no longer come from point-sources, against which retaliation would be possible. Having de-emphasised the military function of nuclear weapons, India has refrained from weaponising its nuclear arsenal and has kept it under strict civilian control.

Nonetheless, contested borders with China are thought to be a key flashpoint of a potentially nuclear Sino-Indian conflict. Regarding the situation with Pakistan, the apprehension in both India and abroad is that any conflict over Kashmir or the culmination of an asymmetric war with India could trigger a nuclear war. But given the retaliatory capacity of both countries, deterrence is likely to hold in the foreseeable future.

As the strategic environment and other states' arsenals evolve, the level of "minimal" deterrence capability may rise as well. Many have proposed that India needs to ready its arsenal to increase the credibility of its deterrence capacity.

However, such an act would also increase China's and Pakistan's threat perceptions, compelling them to further develop and perhaps deploy nuclear weapons, triggering an Asian arms race.

In order to be prepared for the challenges posed by surprise nuclear attacks, India considered creating a National Missile Defence (NMD) capacity. However, the viability of such a capacity, even in the long-term, is questionable. Besides the discouragingly high costs involved, such a defence system has the potential to expand its conflict capability to the seas and even into space in the form of sea and *space-based* missile defence – a surefire way to trigger an arms race.

Space Policy

Space-based infrastructure has simultaneous civilian and military purposes. No state has weaponised (i.e. placed offensive weapons in) space as yet, though the prospect exists. Solar Power Satellites (SPS) hold great potential for the future of energy harvesting and production and may be the most cost-effective method of harnessing solar power in the long term.

India's current edge in the production and deployment of satellites may well give it a strategic advantage in the development of SPS. However, any space-based infrastructure, military or otherwise, may be exposed to major vulnerabilities, namely destruction by lasers, ballistic missiles, crashes, and even a hit by debris

Technology and Information in Military Affairs

Network-Centric Warfare (NCW) uses information and communications technologies to enable military commanders to cope with increasingly complex battlefield situations. A revolutionary development in weaponry is Precision-Guided Munitions (PGMs), weapons guided by computers and space-based infrastructures that can hit long distance targets with pinpoint accuracy. Many argue that PGMs will render obsolete the conventional ballistics-based hardware of traditional military might.

These developments bring to the fore the growing importance of information, military cultural changes, space-based infrastructure, and other technology As the world's leading military powers adopt network-centric tactical doctrines, any nation that lags behind in developing a networked, agile, and flexible military force does so at its own peril and will remain at the losing end of an asymmetry in capacities.

Emerging India and Strategic Culture

The politico-strategic formulation of India's foreign policy has failed to keep up with the rising global activism of its economy, its strategic culture being more reactive than proactive.

This reactive stance stems partly from the lack of a specified, articulated, and coherent global vision of power acquisition and projection. Since independence, India's leadership has published few comprehensive strategic documents. Long-term planning has been relegated in favour of more near-term thinking. India's primary strategic goals have focused on more proximate and short-term matters.

This myopic approach has soured many of India's bilateral relations in the subcontinent and severely impeded its ambition to be recognised as a leading world power.

As India's global economic, political, and strategic presence gains prominence, and challenges to its security increase, the persistence of such a reactive, myopic strategy will prove counter-productive. Though certain issues beyond India's control will, quite naturally, define certain aspects of the global strategic environment, it will still be India's responsibility, as a credible global power, to *contribute* to that strategic environment as well as to the *definition* of what makes a power 'great.' India can start by playing a more active role in global governance.

As part of this exercise, India should articulate an adaptive yet coherent National Strategy that would define India's goals and vision of its role in the world, and thereafter, lay the path towards their realisation.

Micro-Macro Interactions

Globalisation has empowered individuals, groups, and states differently in their respective domains. Complexity—the ever-growing interconnectivity, interactivity and change on multiple levels of multiple systems—typifies contingencies on the level of micro-macro interactions.

Frontier Security

The Arunachal Pradesh border issue and the Aksai Chin tangle are the central issues of contention between India and China. A key concern for India is its vast, porous borders that facilitate drugs and weapons trafficking. Issues likely to come to the fore are: the digging of underground tunnels for illegal entry into India; increasingly complex maritime security; and *space* as a realm of national sovereignty. What further complicates the problems is the decentralisation—by market forces —of power away from governments and nation-states, redefining the very meaning of 'borders.'

Technological Drivers of Conflict

With the increasing reliance on communications technologies for military, business, and even social operations throughout the globe, the incidence and threat of *cyber-warfare,* and the use of computers and the internet as offensive tools loom large. Cyber-warfare attacks can take two key forms: (1) attacks targeting control systems; and (2) attacks targeting data. There is also the threat of cyber-espionage against Indian government databases and information repositories, both classified and unclassified, military and civilian.

With the growing importance of information and the emergence of new technologies facilitating access to it, issues related to *intelligence*, *privacy, identity-theft*, and *intellectual property rights* will gain prominence. Moreover, as information becomes the backbone of more and more social, military and, economic activities, tussles over the *ownership* of information and its usage—i.e. intellectual property rights—could well become the sources of legal, political, and physical conflicts.

In the longer term, the human race will witness seismic shifts in the nature of technology, which would include the convergence of four major realms of technology: Nanotechnology, Biotechnology, Information Technology, and Cognitive/Neuro Technology (NBIC convergence, or converging technologies). Converging technologies have the potential to alter the interaction among man, machine, and matter and, in turn, to alter the very essence of human existence. Polarisation between humans and 'post-humans' in the coming century, and the conflict that emerges therefrom, may well bring about a paradigm shift in the whole concept of global society.

The Environment, Climate Change and National Security

Environmental issues have long had a profound effect on Indian security, but they have taken on another dimension with the *global climate crisis.* In the Indian subcontinent in particular, the manifestations of climate change will threaten scientific, geographic, human, and even national security. Rising temperatures, extremes and anomalies in weather and rising sea levels will lead to desertification, diminution of agricultural and economic output, massive migration and conflicts over resources.

The Himalayan glaciers, already melting fast, may cause unprecedented floods in the northern Indian rivers in the coming years, to be followed in later years by highly depleted river water flows. The river water issue is at the core of the Kashmir problem between India and Pakistan. Regarding Nepal, the sharing and joint management of water resources with India is an issue of particular concern and, vis-à-vis Bangladesh, migration from that country, due to economic and climatic reasons, could adversely impact the region.

Domestically and locally, water has long been a contentious issue and an igniter of conflict at both the local and inter-state levels. The threat of China diverting Tibetan river waters in order to compensate for domestic deficits is of great concern to India, as it would hugely deplete its water sources, leading to water famine situation in the north and threatening its relations with neighbouring countries.

Conflicts and wars over resources such as water are often cloaked in the guise of identity or ideology-based conflicts. The occurrence of resource-based conflicts is rarely overt and is often difficult to discern. Thus, resource issues serve as multipliers, if not igniters, of political conflict.

Economics in the Realm of Security

India's projected global 'rise' can be credited to the fact that, next to China, it has the second highest economic growth rate in the world. But if India's growth and resultant global economic clout fail to keep it afloat or ahead of potential rivals, the latter may usurp India's political and diplomatic position.

Mismanaged aid and development money given to targeted regions can often have the unintended consequences of financing leaders and propagating insurgencies. Due in large part to intertwined licit and illicit activity, whole sectors of employment and entire economies thrive in conflict.

The Military-Industrial Complex (MIC) refers to a coupling of the military, industry and the government that produces a self-reinforcing cycle in which the government supports military development, which, in turn, supports the defence industry, which financially supports the government (often by lobbying politicians), continuing a harmful cycle. While an MIC situation has not yet occurred in India, its emergence can enable military industries to exert unwarranted influence on the government's decision-making.

Investment patterns that encourage urban development and neglect rural areas undergo cycles that reinforce themselves. In rural areas, economic opportunities are scant, resulting in a lack of development and infrastructure. This deficit deters further investment in rural areas, compelling migration to urban areas. Then, as there are even fewer people left in rural areas, there is even less incentive to invest in them, causing further migration to cities. This has the end effect of rural areas remaining stagnant and underdeveloped, while their residents emigrate. This lack of development attention can lead to overt conflict against a seemingly negligent and ineffective state. In urban areas, when poor infrastructure, insufficient capacities, and other problems associated with excessive and increasing urbanisation are compounded with identity-based grievances, a volatile situation arises that may well lead to violence.

Ultimately, the stratification of Indian society based on economic disparities will lead to class hostility and hasten sub-national conflict. Beyond direct conflict driven by poverty itself, the space of opportunity opens up for sub-national groups and state-actors to exploit the impoverished and despairing populace. Further economic stratification in India is likely to surface along three major divides: (1) the regional level (economic divides between various regions of India); (2) urban-rural divide (economic divides between urban and rural populations); and (3) urban poverty (economic divides within single localities).

The Nation and the State in the 21st Century: Perceptions at the Micro-Macro Levels

In the light of a global 'crisis of authority' in which traditional sources of authority have become unable to frame, and act upon, goals, and populations have become disillusioned with conventional centres of power, new sources of authority arise.

In India, much of the void of electoral politics and state structures has been filled by sub-groupism and the reinvocation of traditional and historical global allegiances, information about which has been spread by new technologies—major cases being the rise of pan-Islamism, 'Hindutva' politics, sub-national and nativist movements, and diaspora empowerment.

These factors compound to create perhaps the ultimate challenge that India faces: reconciling the politico-geographic *state* with an identity-based *nation*. The central task for those empowered to deal with the security and integrity of India and its population will be to uphold, strengthen and execute measures necessary to keep the idea—or ideal—of India as one united nation as credible and cohesive as possible.

Conclusion: Managing Security in a Complex Age

A Complex Era

Emerging security threats are highly complex: networked and interactive, and dynamic and evolving. Moreover, individuals, groups, states, and international systems are highly *adaptive with* the evolving circumstances of the systems in which they exist. Change itself is becoming the norm. Lone threats can have interactive consequences and can feed upon one another, serving as *threat multipliers*.

An Evolutionary Systems View of National Security

With the possibility of security threats emerging from multiple sources—civil society, governance, science, economics, technology, the environment, politics, resources, health—a military-centric view of security is obsolete, insufficient and counter-productive in this emerging era.

What is needed today is an evolutionary conception of security that embraces change, dynamic, legitimate demands for justice, as well as the safety of a cohesive nation, all held together by the effective apparatuses of the state.

Rather than merely articulating a set of prioritised threats in need of attention, a genuine understanding of national security needs must contain in its ambit the ability to view the world as a complex, evolving system of systems. Therein, national strategy must align perceived threats and opportunities from multiple sources with capacities of multiple sources.

Foresight and Action: Anticipation and Networked Management

Linear models have defined governance till now. The future has been seen as a simple extension of the past; governments today have been organised to deal with the same problems as yesterday, and tomorrow's problems are expected to be the same as those of today.

The time has come to *anticipate* non-linear challenges by understanding the drivers, trends, potential events, and weak signals—anomalous entities that may become pervasive—that will shape the emerging strategic environment. Strategic thinking, planning, and policy-making must be informed by *diverse* groups of thinkers in order to generate more creative analyses.

Stove-piped, hierarchical solutions are not appropriate for problems that do not easily fit into boxes. Networked solutions to networked problems require *networked management*. The integration of different bureaucracies must be enabled and encouraged at the *operational* level. Rapid communication and coordination between disciplines are necessary when dealing with complex problems.

Conclusion

A whole-scale reform of governance is necessary if India is to effectively address the myriad challenges it faces. Such a reform must engage key individuals from federal, state and municipal government bodies; academia and private sector organisations; the leadership of all political parties and key bureaucrats; and, most importantly, civil society, to create the necessary political will and ensure democratic oversight of the process.

Introduction

In recent decades the world has undergone shifts in economic and political power due in part to new technologies. This new age has been described by various observers as an era of "fragmegration,"[1] "glocalisation,"[2] "the network age,"[3] and "the age of complexity."[4]

At the forefront of this era is the simultaneous occurrence of socio-political integration and fragmentation. It has witnessed the concurrent occurrences of all the following: both global economic interdependence and a rise in protectionism; a proliferation of networked organisations and the fragmentation of groups; trans-national governance as well as an increase in regionalism; a surge in democratic governance backed by civil society and, equally, a rise in extremism; an increase in nationalism and an empowerment of sub- and non-national identities; a cessation of some enmities and increases in others; increases in wealth and increasing disparity in its distribution; rapid advances and dissemination of technology; the privatisation of government services; and global shifts in economic and military power .[5]

When integrative and fragmenting processes emerge at once, constant change emerges. Challenges to the idea of national sovereignty and to the 'integrity' of states have become more commonplace, but have brought with them immense benefits and opportunities. Certain instruments of power—financial, governance, communications, military force, etc—are no longer under the exclusive control of the state. The idea of *sovereignty* has undergone major redefinitions and, given the interaction of social, technological, military, and economic drivers, may continue to do so.

And while the role of the state in global and domestic politics has certainly changed, in the *democratic* Republic of India, the idea and definition of the *nation* also remains contested. The questioning of the legitimacy and credibility of the state in delivering to its citizens comes with nothing less than the potential for the nation itself coming apart, posing perhaps *the* greatest threat to national security that India faces. Challenges to this ability can come from multiple sources: internal and local, external and global, and their compounding mix.

India's often-cited global 'rise' is of central consideration, particularly with regards to the challenges it faces in a global era. However, India's emerging political environment must be a product of both what it confronts *and what it creates*. A strategic culture in which India rises to the occasions that India itself defines is necessary.

In the past, national security spelt physical or geographic protection and was, thus, largely equated with national defence. But this new era has broadened the ability of security challenges to come from diverse sources—economic, environmental, social, technological, and otherwise. Accordingly, there is a need for a new understanding of security, a broadened concept that encompasses the recognition of an array of potential sources of conflict, as well as the reality of change and the possibilities, not the mere limitations, of global and local systems.

While the course of events for individuals, states, and societies was once thought of as linear, predictable extensions of history, the highly *networked*, interconnected nature of threats makes the systems of challenges that India faces inherently *non-linear*. A small event localised to one part of a system could lead to large scale consequences for the whole, while a large event in a system may have just a minor effect.

The drivers of this non-linear change are many and may seem even paradoxical. These drivers, in the form of integrative and fragmenting processes, occur simultaneously at different scales: the *micro* level, that of individuals and groups; the *macro* level: nation-states and global systems and; *micro-macro interactions*, the nexus between these two.[6]

In India, the micro level is largely typified by the central role of perception, increased reliance on the *network* form of organisation to facilitate communications, as well as systemic problems in governance and service provision. The macro level is characterised by new modes of perception and technologies that affect the international system, as well as a new global role for India— a role that it must both assume and create. Between these two levels, a number of compounding, interactive threats emerge, requiring an approach to security management that factors in *complexity*, the increase in interdependence, connectivity and constant change in systems.

This paper will present an overview of some of the key structural shifts and drivers of change in each system of analysis, while providing scenarios that could result from the interactions of a few drivers and proposing policy and practical alternatives. The paper samples from a wide array of innovative literature in an analysis that aims to fill the gaps in the existing body.

The key focus is conceptual shifts in the nature of conflict. They include the threat posed by networked forms of organisation; the heightened role of information and perceptions in both shaping and resolving conflicts; examination of deficits in governance as a security threat; emerging challenges in nuclear, space, and military strategies; global shifts in geopolitical power and their effects on Indian strategic thinking; the security implications of emerging technologies, climate change and the environment; economics; and emerging global identity mediation.

The paper concludes by proposing a new paradigm for conceptualising, framing and acting on national security: an evolutionary systems view of security that employs networked management and anticipatory governance in a complex era. It recommends a comprehensive reform of India's national security system in the light of emerging challenges and opportunities.

Micro Level Challenges

The information and technological revolution of the 1990s has changed the way people are able to communicate and organise themselves. An increased level of connectivity brought on by this revolution, through such technologies as the internet and mobile phones, has diminished the barriers of space and time, in turn, expediting change and exchange in systems of all sorts.[7] These changes have been felt in the environments in which states perform, and within states themselves. Actors within and across organisations have been empowered manifold, due largely to the increased number of connections and amount of information to which they have access.

Individuals and groups—the *micro* level of global political structures—have arguably benefited the most from these organisational changes. While global politics was once seen as an extension of nation-state and government activity, the pressures that individuals and groups are able to exert on sub-national, national, and even international systems have in many ways changed the nature of the game. In the light of this decentralisation of power, bolstered further by privatisation and economic liberalisation, "*government*" increasingly gives way to the much more encompassing "*governance*".[8]

Information itself has become a foundational element of an economic revolution, the "knowledge economy," and the transmission of information has become the backbone of a new social order. And it is fundamentally information, its communication, and the distribution of its control[9] that has altered conventional power structures.

The Information Revolution and the Role of Perception

As information increases in importance, the role of *perceptions*—subjectively and inter-subjectively processed and contextualised information—has heightened immensely.

Security itself can be understood as the *perceived* confidence in the current or future state of affairs. Conflict and other 'threats to security' often emerge as reactions to a *deficit* in this perceived confidence on the personal, collective, or state levels. Perceptions can spread through populations, bringing about enmity and causing groups to lose faith in some element of the status quo. Negative or otherwise incongruent perceptions can be harbingers of conflict and violence. Perceptions can either be driven by legitimate conditions and 'facts' or initiated by politics, agendas, and fictions.

Security dilemmas, most often discussed with regards to international politics,[10] also occur on the micro scale between individuals and groups. Perceived offence by one party causes the other to build up its own protective measures; the latter are perceived as a threat to the other party, and a cycle continues until a threshold of enmity is reached and conflict arises. Communal tension is perhaps the most prominent example in the Indian domestic context, in which communal groups fear the intentions of the other, due in large part to minimal communication and other interlinkages between the groups.[11] But such dilemmas can extend to state-sub-state, native-migrant, and other ostensibly competitive relations.

Tied to the issue of perceptions and security dilemmas are information cascades: every subsequent actor, based on the observations of others, makes the same choice as his or her neighbours, independent of his or her private decision. In an informational cascade, each agent acts according to individual compulsions that are influenced by social considerations. With new forms of media, perceptions can cascade across geographic space, facilitated by information technologies that connect geographically disparate groups. In 1992 and 1993, the enmity engendered by events in Ayodhya, Uttar Pradesh, spread to Mumbai; while attacks on churches in the eastern state of Orissa in 2008 were soon followed by attacks on churches as far away as Karnataka, though the locations were geographically separate.

Identity

In recent years, the credibility of traditional sources of power (particularly the state) has declined. In its wake, new sources of authority and allegiance have emerged. Diverse *identities*—born from the ways in which individual and collective affiliation are perceived, defined and acted upon—have come to the forefront of social and political affairs.

India's history has long been influenced by identity-based conflicts, whether they be the ethno-linguistic federal movements of the late 1940s and 1950s, nativist movements in places like Maharashtra and the northeast, class issues in the Naxal corridor, or inter-religious strife. In the 1990s and 2000s, identity politics in India has largely taken the form of religion. The destruction of the Babri Masjid in Ayodhya in 1992, and bombings, riots and terrorist attacks throughout the country since then have mainly been seen through the lens of inter-religious conflict. Many[12] have attributed this to what Samuel Huntington has referred to as a "Clash of Civilizations," the notion that conflicts in the 21st century will be fought along the lines of civilisation, which are largely co-terminous with those of religion. As Huntington has articulated,

> The great divisions among humankind and the dominating source of conflict will be cultural... The principal conflicts of global politics will occur between nations and groups of different civilizations. The clash of civilizations will dominate global politics. The fault lines between civilizations will be the battle lines of the future...At the micro-level, adjacent groups along the fault lines between civilizations struggle, often violently, over the control of territory and each other.[13]

If this thesis appears correct, part of its accuracy can be attributed to the self-fulfilling nature of this prophecy and those like it.[14] If a few incidents align with the prediction, the prediction is thought to be accurate. Accordingly, many will view society through the 'civilisational' framework, and, in turn, fear an escalation of the same sort of violence. What was once a conjecture turns into a policy prescription and, thereafter, a feedback cycle of perceptions unfurls. In the case of Hindu-Muslim tensions, for example[15], a small group of Hindus distrust Muslims and attack the latter; a slightly larger group of Muslims, fearing escalation, retaliate. Then, still more Hindus feel greater resentment and retaliate further, and the wheels of hostility start to turn until such views spread beyond groups to whole, increasingly divided, distinct communities. Distrust and enmity feed upon, and reinforce, one another.

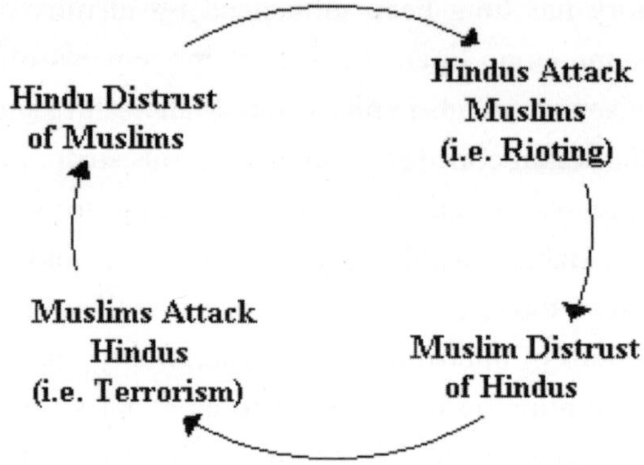

In the process, the diversity of each community is weakened, and each group solidifies its own perceptions of the 'other,' reinforcing the 'other's' perception of itself. Previously heterogeneous 'Hindus' abruptly become homogenous in their distrust of what is thought to be a monolithic community of 'Muslims'. In turn, otherwise diverse Muslims become homogeneous in their fear and distrust of Hindus, a group increasingly seen by Muslims as monolithic. The initially established, opposing identities reinforce one another into homogeneity and primacy.

The same juxtapositions and self-fulfilling phenomena can be said of any identity-based categorisations, whether ethno-linguistic, religious, class, caste, national, or otherwise.

Given this diversity of simultaneously occurring identities, Huntington's thesis itself neglects two major factors: (1) the strong interlinkages *across* identities (i.e. a Hindu, a Christian, and a Jew can all be Malayali-speaking Indians); and (2) the divisions *within* each identity that are often as strong as, if not stronger than, those between them (i.e. a Hindu can be a Hindi speaker or a Tamil speaker, or a Muslim can be a Ja'afari Shi'te or a Hanbali Sunni). As Amartya Sen has written in a rebuttal to the "Clash of Civilizations" thesis:

> A person belongs to many different groups, of which a religious affiliation is only one...The increasing tendency to overlook the many identities

> that any human being has and to try to classify individuals according to a single allegedly pre-eminent religious identity is an intellectual confusion that can animate dangerous divisiveness…In fact, of course, the people of the world can be classified according to many other partitions, each of which has some—often far-reaching—relevance in our lives: nationalities, locations, classes, occupations, social status, languages, politics, and many others. While religious categories have received much airing in recent years, they cannot be presumed to obliterate other distinctions, and even less can they be seen as the only relevant system of classifying people across the globe.[16]

Identities are rarely monolithic. Indeed, the key challenge of identity politics is that *identity and its purpose can be easily fluid and dynamic, expanding and retracting in inclusivity as contexts and political tidings warrant*. Put simply, single resolutions to the challenges of identity politics can be insufficient as contexts and identities themselves change.[17]

Perception Management and Perception Influence

Perception management refers to the proactive modes of influencing the emotions, motives, and reasoning of a target audience within a broader strategy. While government-based propaganda was initially the main tier of perception management and other 'psychological operations', the proliferation of media outlets and decentralisation of perception control modes make the realm of perception far more complex. Mobile phones, news media, websites, and social networks contribute to the diffusion of perceptions, and all serve as modes of managing perceptions.

Wars and battles in which information is the main weapon, battleground and goal, the phenomenon known as "information warfare" will become increasingly prominent in the future. As John Arquilla and David Ronfeldt write, "Adversaries are learning to emphasize 'information operations' and 'perception management'—that is, media-oriented measures that aim to attract or disorient rather than coerce, and that affect how secure a society, a military, or other actor feels about its knowledge of itself and of its adversaries. Psychological disruption may become as important a goal as physical destruction."[18]

In many ways, the *democratic* state faces the biggest challenge in the realm of perception management. Sub-national and non-national adversaries, their activities and, thus, the perceptions of their activities are easily adaptable and even disposable as situations warrant. If, for example, an insurgent or a terrorist group is losing an ideological battle, it can easily assume a new name and project new collective identities in order to make the political landscape more favourable. On the other hand, the state as a central authority does not have such liberty of action. As the ultimate sovereign and hegemon, the state's role comes with great constraints as well as opportunities in the realm of perception management.

In a democratic system of governance, perceptions take on a peculiar role. Indeed, it is the very *purpose* of democracy to secure the value, representation, and accommodation of diverse, possibly fluctuating perceptions.

As access to different information itself increases, the rate of *change* of perceptions, their political consequences and manifestations, will also increase in unprecedented ways. The evolution of perceptions is something that democracies are particularly well structured to manage. In a democracy, a change in perceptions will be reflected in civil society, and a change of government (via the electoral system) and other structures of governance. But India's specific *systems* of democracy face new challenges as these systems may not be able to cope effectively with the altered *rate* of perception changes. Accordingly, these democratic systems—particularly those of the state rather than civil society—may not be able to accommodate the increasing diversity of evolving views with those disillusioned by the process and seeking alternatives.[19] This is particularly true as new social networks (described below) evolve and serve as their own vehicles of perception management.

Networked Organisation

Both a cause and effect of the empowerment of individuals and groups is the rise of *networks* as a form of managing information, resources, and capital. *Networks* in this context refer to *highly decentralised and distributed forms of social organisation comprising the links between nodes* (the agents in a network). Networks often transcend and circumvent formal hierarchical organisational structures.

Network Structures

William Evan has described three mains types of network structure: the "chain" network, in which information or resources are carried across a line of separated contacts and communication is facilitated through intermediary nodes; the "star-hub" network, in which actors are connected to a central node, and must go through that central *hub* to communicate with one another and; the "all-channel" network, in which each node is connected to all the others.[20] Most social networks are often some hybrid of the three, depending on the type, *purpose* and organisational needs of the network itself.

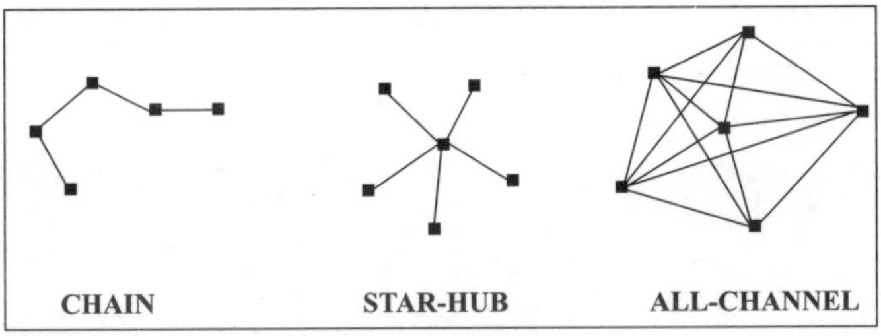

Due to the nature and qualities of certain actors, some nodes are more connected than others. These are referred to as *hubs*. Highly connected hubs have access to the diverse information and resources of the many nodes with which they are connected; they also serve as intermediaries between many other nodes. Hubs may have a disproportionately important role in a network, because a single change in the hub, or an innovation adopted by the hub can easily spread to the connected nodes.

Agents in social networks tend to *cluster*, form cliques or small groups based on exceptionally high degrees of connectivity, or *strong ties*.[21] Agents in clusters have collective access to the same information and experiences.

Weak ties, on the other hand, are those that are contingent on lesser degrees of trust, and connect otherwise disparate or distant clusters. As weak ties connect clusters that otherwise have access to different information and

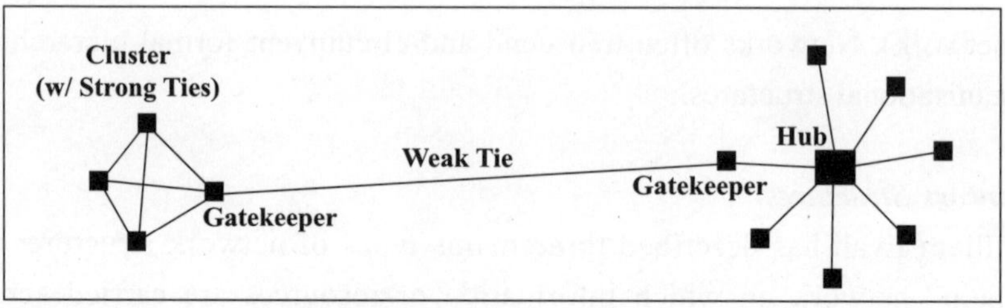

resources, they are often conduits of large-scale communication, innovation and change.[22] *Gatekeepers*, in turn, are those agents that connect long-distance clusters through weak ties.

In Fig A, the cliques are independent; there are no connections between any of them. Accordingly, when a piece of information (represented in grey), with its source at Node X (the node at the bottom right) is spread, it can only be shared with the other nodes in the clique.

Fig A

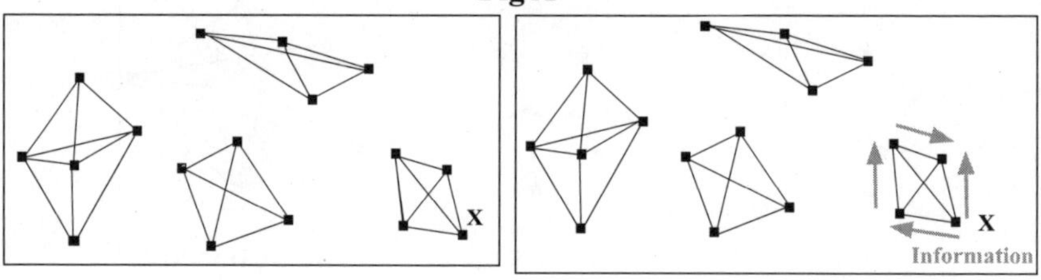

Unconnected Clusters Minimal Information Flow

In Fig. B, the cliques are connected by a single weak tie each (in thick black). When information has its source at Node X, it can be shared with other cliques more extensively through the weak ties that bridge them. In this case, the information can spread to *all* the cliques, albeit gradually.

Fig B

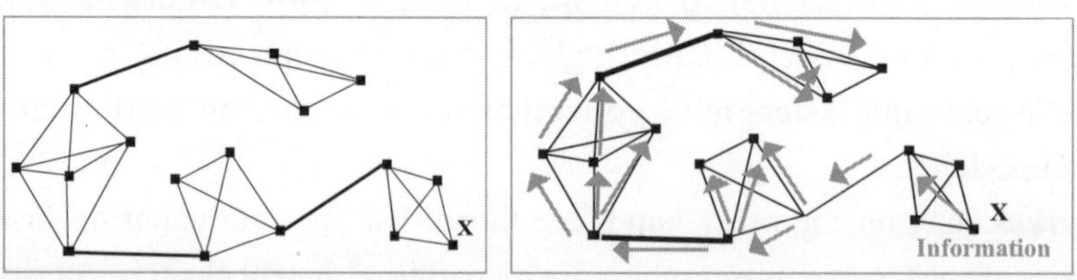

Clusters Connected by a Few Weak Ties Enhanced Degree of Information Flow

Lastly, in Fig C, a number of weak ties are added (in dotted), connecting all of the cliques in a number of different places. When information with its source at Node X is shared, the information can be spread to all cliques rapidly, and through a number of different avenues.

Fig C

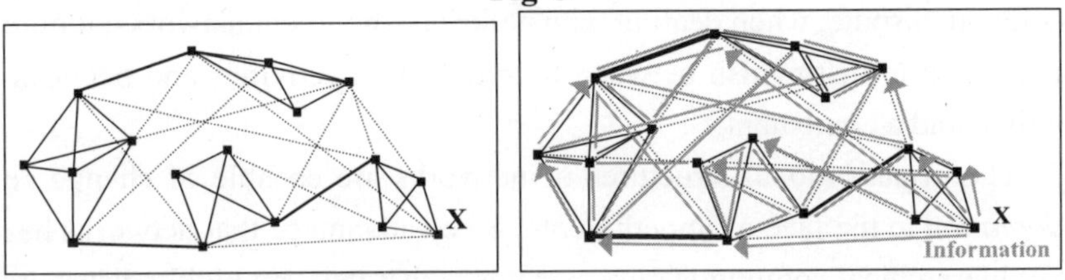

Clusters Connected by Many Weak Ties High Degree of Information Flow

Communication in Networks

The relationships between nodes in a network are modes of communication of information, or transfer of capital. Networks are used to communicate at either short or long distances, depending on the type of link. *Cascades* and *contagion* refer to the way that an innovation, idea, or a piece of information can spread through a whole network from a single source or catalyst. A cascade will occur as other agents react to their neighbours' change by adapting themselves, with huge effects on whole systems. For example, a contagious disease in a single person can, through contact, spread across a population.[23]

Swarming refers to "a behavior in which autonomous, or semi-autonomous, units of action converge on a focal point from several different directions, and thereafter regroup."[24] Swarming is behaviour particular to networks, as communication between, and self-organisation of, the nodes is often abrupt and spontaneous, rather than hierarchically mandated.

Networks are either *designed*, created or self-organised with a specific intent in mind; or *emergent*, resulting organically from multiple individual interactions and aims. Designed networks tend towards structures—organisational features, narratives, and operational doctrines—that reinforce their primary *purpose*, while considering structural challenges such as resource availability or external opposition. Emergent networks, on the other hand, are shaped by the needs of individual actors, and organically form supra structures that emphasise key nodes (such as hubs) and patterns.

Networks may extend in all directions, making a definitive start and end difficult to pin-point. Where a single network begins and a second one starts is often in dispute; when dealing with nefarious or violent networks, it might be difficult to distinguish between licit and illicit activities and between a civilian and a combatant.

The organisational structures of networks are capable of change and *adaptation* in the face of impediments. A key advantage that networks have over hierarchical communication systems is that they are highly distributed and decentralied, lacking a central head whose demise would otherwise destroy the whole network. As Phil Williams has written of criminal networks:

> Many…networks are inherently dispersed, with the result that they *do not provide obvious centers of gravity* or loci for law enforcement attacks. Lacking a physical infrastructure or a large investment of sunk costs that would add significantly to their vulnerability, networks can also migrate easily from areas where risks from law enforcement are high to areas where risks are much lower.[25]

Due to distribution of power, as well as redundant distribution of information and access, networks are highly resilient to attacks and other challenges. If a single node or group of nodes is compromised, others may compensate for the deficit.

Moreover, both individual agents and aggregate networks are highly *adaptive*, altering both their internal composition and external relations with structural changes and constraints.

These characteristics apply to social and other networks of all sorts, whether they are affiliated with technologies, religious extremist, ideological and nationalist groups, economic transactions, trafficking, and organised crime.

Information and Communications Technologies

A reduction of transmission time and cost of communication—due to even commercially available mobile technologies—has increased the level and amount of communication the world over. An increasing number of individuals are able to connect with one another directly and immediately, across geographic borders and distances, facilitating the development and maintenance of non-hierarchical, long-distance social networks. As Jessica Matthews has written,

> Information technologies "disrupt hierarchies" and spread power among more people and groups. For drastically lowering the costs of communication, consultation, and coordination [information technologies], decentralised networks are favoured over other modes of organisation. In a network, individuals or groups link for joint action without building a physical or formal institutional presence.[26]

When coupled with face-to-face social organisation, mobile technologies enable more long-distance *weak ties*. This has the effect of spreading change more rapidly and across both geographic and social boundaries.

In addition to increasing communication rates through modes such as e-mail, the internet has provided forums for social organisation and management in a wholly different realm. Websites are able to transfer information to a large audience from any source, at minimal cost to the broadcaster. With greater access to broadcasting and communications forums, dissemination and processing of information occurs at increasingly rapid paces.

Mobile communications networks enable what Howard Rheingold has referred to as *smart-mobs*.[27] A smart-mob is a "self-structuring and self-organizing set of people who…can spontaneously form into a group that is controlled by no single person, yet which moves as if it has a mind of its own. Since mobile text-messages can be instantly forwarded like e-mail pass-arounds, the mobs frequently involve masses of people who may have never even met."[28] A smart-mob can behave intelligently because of exponentially increasing network links, enabling people to connect to information and to others.[29]

Communications technologies, in both hierarchical forms (i.e. a single source or group of sources of information) and networked forms (i.e. decentralised modes of information sharing) also serve as powerful forms of *perception management*. Ideas or processed and framed pieces of information can be projected to an audience and disseminated on a much larger scale and more rapid rate than previously possible, shaping the way that large numbers of people view and react to events.

Control, Power, and Perception in Networks[30]

While conventional analysis tends to focus on individuals and their capabilities, network theory posits that it is the *relationships* between things—rather than the things themselves—that are important in understanding what results from their interaction. Analysing networks enables an understanding of the important relationships, the key areas of influence within an organisation, and what gives organisations their strength.

Hubs (highly connected agents) often control access to other agents in a network, and tend to be central sharing points of information and resources; thus, they are often centres of power within networks. Likewise, *gatekeepers* (conduits of long-distance ties) bridge otherwise disconnected groups. Accordingly, gatekeepers can either enable or disable communication between different clusters, and are key agents in their own right.

If gatekeepers or hubs are removed or otherwise compromised, a network will fragment into disconnected parts. Thus, these two types of agents become central points of strength or failure.

But what appears to be a hub from a small scale may be a less meaningful agent when viewed in the larger context. The organisational reach of the networked group, as well as the purpose of the analysis will determine the scale of analysis that is required.

Mapping relationships within networks enables an understanding of the inner workings of an organisation—those that go beyond formal command structures. Thereafter, those who understand the informal power structures of a system can use the existing dynamics to influence the system as a whole; to disrupt nefarious flows or enable even small catalysts to make large changes. For example, because hubs are main sharers of information, altering the information that the hub receives will affect the rest of the network.

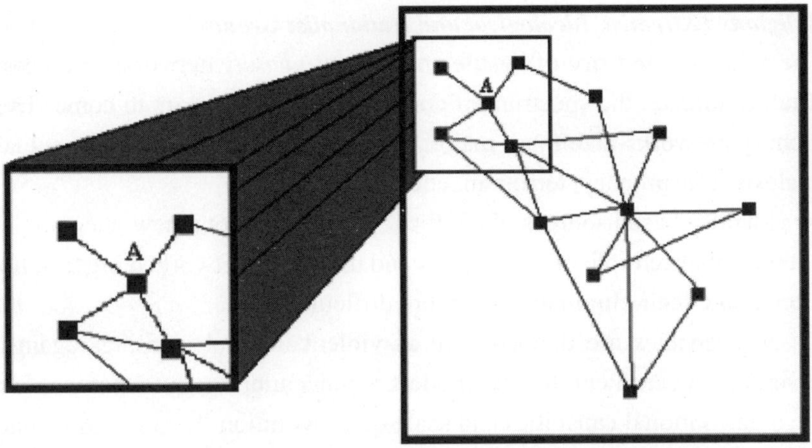

In this figure, on the left, node A appears to be the central hub. But seen in the larger context (right), that is not the case.

However, because networks contain links that can extend across geography, *control* of whole networks is fundamentally impossible. While hubs and gatekeepers can influence certain regions of a network, they too can adapt, be made redundant, even circumvented. The removal of even a few key nodes does not necessarily spell the end of a connected network. Networks in which gatekeepers or hubs are made redundant (i.e. there are other nodes serving similar purposes) will be less centralised. A less centralised network will have fewer points of failure, and will be more resilient in the wake of disruption. Moreover, because networks are highly adaptive, if a central node is disrupted, the others can easily alter their structures to compensate for the lost.

Ultimately, the primary mode of influence in a network is the common narrative—the shared, institutionalised perception that brings the agents in a network together. Networks are often based on different types and degrees of connectivity. Relationships that are based on common ethnic or linguistic ties, for example, will be different from those based on economic transactions.

A common narrative or identity shapes the way that agents in a network frame, process, and share information within the network. Influence over the narrative of a network will fundamentally determine influence within the network as a whole.

Religious Extremist, Ideological and Nationalist Groups

The existence and rise of hostile and violent *identity* networks will colour, if not dominate, the spectrum of conflict in India for years to come. These identity networks take three major forms that are not necessarily mutually exclusive: insurgency, terrorism, and communalism.

Identity-based sources of conflict are certainly not a new phenomenon, but the enhanced role of perceptions and the use of networked organisations often make their elimination far more difficult.

Insurgencies are defined here as violent internal uprisings against a sovereign government that has modest popular support, but otherwise lacks the organisational capacities and scale of a revolution.[31]

Insurgencies have emerged in various places throughout India, namely the northeast, where insurgency has been waged by a number of sub-national groups representing a variety of ethnic groups, causes, and demands; Kashmir, which has had local popular elements supported heavily by Pakistani factions; and the Naxal Movement that has gripped much of eastern and central India. These insurgencies may expand in depth and scale, while others may arise based on socio-political and economic factors that enable them.

Solutions to security and conflict problems certainly take military forms.[32] But the excessive use of military force often comes with immense political fallout. As the authors of a RAND Corporation report on *How Terrorist Groups End* state:

> There is no battlefield solution to terrorism. Military force usually has the opposite effect from what is intended: it is often overused, alienates the local population by its heavy-handed nature, and provides a window of opportunity for terrorist-group recruitment.[33]

Moreover, the credibility of the military force amongst affected populations can have a meaningful impact on the success of the operation itself. If a military force is seen as favourable to local non-combatant populations, the latter would support the aims and efforts of the former. If seen as unfavourable, the force can upset local populations and bolster the cause of the adversaries.

Networks have empowered smaller-scale groups in their organisational flexibility. Decapitation—or the removal of the head or leader of an organisation—may change nothing if the organisation itself is decentralised command and authority do not rest on single agents, and communications are made redundant: the organisation as a whole can adapt to the situation with great ease. Splitting the leadership of an adversarial organisation is a tactic promoted by various thinkers[34] in order to weaken its cohesive strength. However, this would create multiple organisations operating independently. Though the new, smaller groups will have less operational power, their factionalisation will add complexity to the task of dealing with them. A single, more monolithic unit is often more easy to influence.

The tactic of *terrorism* and its highly decentralised networked strategies are another form that these challenges will take. Terrorism is a highly controversial and political term that plays a major role in perception management. While definitions abound, terrorism is commonly understood as violence or the threat of violence perpetrated by sub-national actors or clandestine agents against civilian or non-combatant targets, with the intention of influencing a populace toward politically, religiously, or socially-motivated objectives. Any collective body such as insurgent or communal entities, political groups and organised crime syndicates are capable of employing terrorist tactics.

Terrorism is a particularly efficient political weapon for sub-national actors, given the recent rise in their capacities, their increased demand for autonomy and the asymmetry between their power and that of the state. Indeed, terrorism is often referred to as a "tactic of the weak."

The mode by which organisations that employ terrorism (hereafter referred to as "terrorist organisations") structure themselves, changes markedly depending on the purpose of the group, internal constraints (such as resources), external or structural constraints (such as the capacities of the state) and the conditions of the wider political environment in which they operate.

However, the vulnerability of small-scale hierarchical organisations to infiltration, decapitation, and destruction has led many terrorist groups to adapt network or hybrid organisational structures. In such structures, knowledge, plans, capacities, and authority are distributed, decentralised, and made redundant, in line with many of the characteristics of networks described above. To maintain an element of operational command, hierarchical elements are also often maintained, so that many terrorist organisations have a key group of decision-makers, a second level of 'commanders,' and a larger number of 'foot-soldiers' who organise themselves into cells akin to the 'cliques' of social networks.[35]

Due to the hybrid nature of the organisation, however, the members of various tiers are often hard to distinguish. Likewise, members at all levels of 'command' can comprise ordinary people from the broader society, and are embedded in even non-nefarious social networks, making it difficult to draw a line between the combatant 'terrorist' and the non-combatant civilian.

This fluidity and distribution provide the terrorist organisation one of its most powerful assets: organisational learning and adaptation. In case of infiltration or capture by law enforcement or intelligence agencies, a terrorist organisation will need to swiftly adapt its modes of action and information set-up. As a recent RAND Corporation report on organisational learning in terror groups has articulated:

> When a terrorist group can learn—and learn well—it can act systematically to fulfill its needs, strengthen its capabilities, and advance its strategic agenda. The ability to learn allows a terrorist group to purposefully adapt to ever-evolving circumstances… A terrorist group's *ability to learn is,* therefore, *a primary determinant of the level of threat it poses*, since learning is the route through which organizations can seek solutions to the problems that bound their freedom of action and limit their ability to pursue their goals in changing operational and security circumstances.[36]

An example of such adaptation is pan-Islamist terrorism. Al Qaeda was once the central hub of a global network that connected various national liberation movements around the world.[37] As the hub of a star-hub network, Al Qaeda facilitated communications between geographically dispersed groups from its bases in Sudan and later in Afghanistan. Such connectivity allowed each local group to share with affiliates around the world, by going through Al Qaeda, the central, coordinating node that managed those communications. Since the US invasion of Afghanistan and its attacks on Al Qaeda infrastructure and its Taliban host, however, local groups have increasingly connected with one another directly, circumventing Al Qaeda as the 'central' facilitator. In the latter situation, if Al Qaeda were fully destroyed, the local groups would still be able to function and communicate effectively, as communications have been made redundant and distributed.[38]

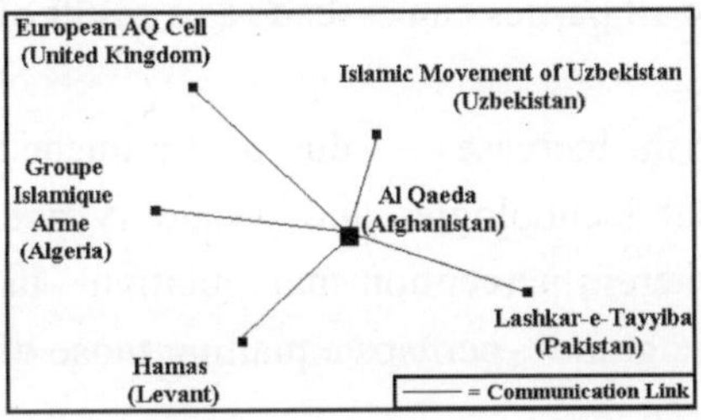

Pre-Adaptation Islamist Terrorism

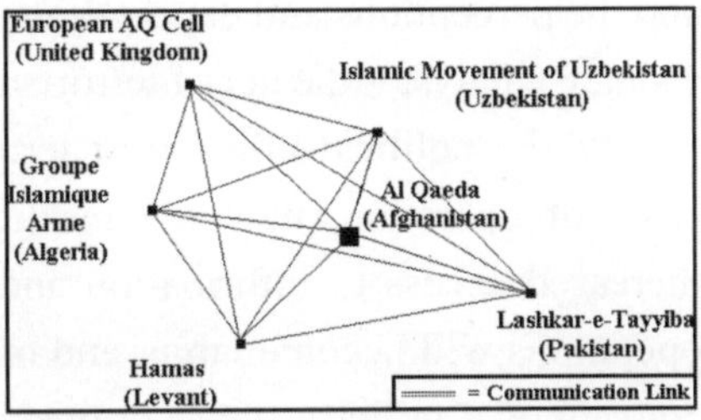

Post-Adaptation Islamist Terrorism

The same is likely for local terrorist groups. Though it may have been facilitated by a central node earlier, these groups' operations, connectivity, and control are becoming increasingly decentralised and distributed. Thus, groups have become so resilient that the destruction of a single node does not necessarily spell the collapse of the whole network.

Adaptive capacities exist not only on the organisational and tactical levels, but also on the political level. Terrorist group objectives and even *raisons d'etre* can evolve according to the changing circumstances. Groups can split into various wings based on ideological divides or environmental changes. If a group's political strategy is not effective, it can easily assume a modified identity under another name and act accordingly.

In line with this notion of changing characters, terrorism has often been spoken of as theatre, with the political objective of influencing a wider audience, rather than mere destructive crime. It can, thus, be thought of as a mode of perception manipulation or perception influence. Unlike more conventional tactics, terrorism generally aims to disrupt rather than merely destroy. A key strategic aim of disruptive terrorist tactics, which often target highly symbolic public spaces, is to manipulate internal security dilemmas between identity-based groups.

Such acts can cause common citizens to fear attacks on basic institutions that serve to bind society together, such as places of worship, transportation systems and work places. The psychological damage inflicted by terrorism—the breakdown in confidence, the fear and the retaliation – is often greater than the physical destruction. It is a process that tends to feed upon itself.[39]

The initial imbalance of perceptions, or security dilemma is manipulated, and the perceptions and expectations of all parties can cascade as a result of a single catalyst – the act of terrorism.

As the political efficacy of terrorism increases — due to diminished costs of operation, new organisational technologies and weaponry and increased access to information and therein perception manipulation—its operations will become larger and more grand—perhaps equalling those of conventional military sieges or operations.

Communal conflict is another related form that identity-based conflict takes. Historically, communal conflict has taken the form of large-scale communal rioting and targeted killings. Materialisation of such conflict often appears spontaneous and takes the form of swarming, in which autonomous units abruptly converge in a single action. 'Smart-mobs', recently bolstered by technological media, are also evident during certain outbreaks of communal conflict. Despite certain organic and spontaneous tendencies of communal conflict, two key enabling factors for communal outbreaks are (1) leadership by key agents, i.e. movement leaders and "riot specialists"[40] who instigate or facilitate incidents; and (2) pre-existing social tension. Violent outbreaks of communalism can pose a particularly virulent threat to Indian identity and, thus, the viability and security of the nation.

To all forms of identity-based conflict, cascading effects are of great relevance. The rapid dissemination of perceptions and violence through social contagion creates a situation where even minor events can catalyse large-scale traumas that have the power to bring down whole systems.

Once the initial shock of a violent incident sets in, it is not easy to mitigate its effects. In fact, incidents of violence undergo *increasing returns*, in which initial tendencies in a system remain, due to their initial advantage, and influence the future development of the system. The enmity between communities grows, making it increasingly difficult to ease the tension, not to speak of bringing about any kind of durable peace.

Economic Networks

Networks based on economic transfers play a four-fold role in creating security challenges: (1) such networks directly finance adversaries and their criminal activities; (2) they detract finances from legitimate concerns; (3) such transactions often represent breaches in the law unto themselves and harm people directly; and (4) they often represent deeper and more intrinsic issues, such as corruption in governance and service provision, etc.

According to various estimates, the black or underground economy accounts for at least 35 percent of the national economy.[41] In India, a key issue of note is the fluidity between licit and illegitimate financial networks. Due to the burdensome legacy of an excessive bureaucracy with its occupational culture of impunity and a number of other factors, many legitimate financial transactions take on illicit and illegitimate aspects. In many ways, the inseparable fusion of the 'black' and 'white' economies of India make it near impossible for the latter to thrive without elements of the former.

Money laundering, offshore banking, and other illicit forms of financial trafficking are three key economic networks that can bridge legal and illegal activity.

Hawala, an "informal, international banking channel that runs alongside the legal one which may be defined as having the sanction from the country's financial authorities,"[42] is an often-cited phenomenon in which the lines between licit and illegal activity are blurred. *Hawala* is used primarily to transfer untaxed money over long distances, and is a highly decentralised set of social and transfer networks, the key nodes of which are referred to as '*hawaladars*.'

Because of the informal nature of *hawala*, there is no fool-proof way to monitor its activities. Accordingly, the *hawala* system has also been used for money laundering from various sources. The connection between *hawala* and terrorist activities has long been established. Indeed,

> the system has proved to be extremely useful for money laundering and masking the intricate financial operations required by terrorists, drug dealers and other criminal elements. Given its size and semi-legitimate status in South Asia, it is not hard for terrorists to transfer money using *Hawala* channels. They are labyrinths replete with pseudonyms, middlemen and dead ends. Wealthy Arab patrons in the Middle East are likely to send funds to al Qaeda through *Hawala* organizations, as do myriad Arab charities acting as fund-raising fronts.[43]

Given the nexus between the activities of various groups, an overlap between the *hawala* system with other decentralised, informal financial systems is likely in the future. *Hawala*, with its roots in the Islamic world, also has parallels in the *fei-ch'ien* of China, *hui kuan* in Hong Kong, the *hundi* system of interest-gathering of even licit transactions in India, *padala* in the Philippines, *phei kwan* in Thailand and others,[44] and may expand its reach through these networks as well.

Narcotics Trafficking

Drug trafficking poses two key threats. First, the trafficked materials cause massive social problems, harm society directly and contribute to the spread of infections such as HIV. Second, narcotics often provide funding for criminal networks, insurgent groups, and others that directly seek to harm India's interests.

India is located between two global hubs of opiate production: the Golden Crescent, the mountainous region between Afghanistan, Pakistan and Iran; and the Golden Triangle, the area between Myanmar (Burma), Laos, Vietnam, Thailand, and arguably Yunnan Province in China.

Domestically, legal production of opium for scientific purposes and as raw material for the production of chemicals such as acetic anhydride is diverted for the illegal production of heroin, mainly in Uttar Pradesh, Madhya Pradesh, and Rajasthan, as well as the Hill Tracts of some states.[45] Organised crime syndicates have been heavily involved in the trafficking of narcotics from the Nepal border region.[46]

Networks of drug-runners throughout the subcontinent extend further afield, creating a global chain that links drugs with the spread of HIV, organised crime, terrorism and money laundering. In his volume on the Al Qaeda terrorist network, Rohan Gunaratna writes that "drugs from Latin America have been exchanged for weapons from the former Soviet Union... while the Paraguayan cartels of Pedro Juan Caballero, the Japanese-Brazilian cartel, the Turkish cartel, and the Chinese Mafia (14-K Triad, Pak Lung Fu) have also been detected of the triple-border region of Latin America."[47] Columbian cocaine money has also been trafficked through underground channels in Mumbai, a phenomenon that was at its peak in the 1990s.[48] The enterprise is global in scale, but affects local jurisdictions immensely and often disproportionately.

Arms Proliferation

India is located amidst a number of receding conflicts that serve as sources of, and conduits for, the proliferation of small arms. Arms trafficking represents a massive threat for internal security. As a recent report by the Commonwealth Human Rights Initiative argues,

> Conflicts today...are fought most often with cheap and portable light weapons...Along with a range of sophisticated and deadly types of light weapons, it is also cheap and abundant throughout zones of conflict. US $50 million, the cost of a modern jet fighter, will purchase enough assault weapons to equip an army of 200,000. Among warlords, rebel organizations, criminal networks, and security forces in the world's poorest regions—South Asia and Sub-Saharan Africa—these are usually the weapons of choice.[49]

According to a report in *Outlook India*, which cited a study by the British Non-Governmental Organisation (NGO) Oxfam, Amnesty International and the International Network on Small Arms (IANSA), large numbers of small arms are manufactured illegally in factories in Bihar and Uttar Pradesh, and sold on the black market for as little as Rs. 200. Many of these factories are operated by India's organised crime syndicates and supply arms to Naxalites, who dominate a long corridor from Andhra Pradesh to Bihar.[50]

While even the present amount of small arms that are being trafficked in South Asia and India pose a substantial threat, the number that may emerge from current, receding, and future regional conflicts and proliferate around the region will compound the threat. The main areas from which arms come are the Afghan-Pakistan border, Sri Lanka and the Liberation Tigers of Tamil Eelam (LTTE) (which has entered the *business* of weapons trafficking), east and northeast India and Nepal, particularly with the projected de-guerrillisation of the Maoist forces. Receding and ongoing conflicts in Afghanistan and Pakistan, the former Soviet Union, Sri Lanka, Nepal, and Southeast Asia leave a massive number of light arms floating around South Asia. These arms either make their way into the hands of citizens and insurgent groups throughout India by market-based economic networks or, intentionally, through the work of the activities of anti-Indian groups such as Pakistan's Inter-Services Intelligence (ISI), the LTTE, and the United Liberation Front of Assam (ULFA).[51]

The role of states and weapons manufacturers in arms proliferation as sources and conduits for arms is, of course, seminal. As part of their political-military strategy, China, Pakistan, and others have provided arms to militants within India's borders.[52] These arms have, following their initial use by organised militants, entered the black 'market' that transfers weapons through the populations at market price. Weapons manufacturers and traffickers often deal directly with sub-national actors, circumventing their conventional nation-state interlocutors[53] if the price is right. These transactions minimise the level of accountability in the flow of arms.

Human Trafficking

The trafficking of persons poses a multi-dimensional threat: (1) individual human security is threatened and the victims, mainly young girls, are raped, enslaved, and otherwise physically and psychologically abused; (2) financial proceeds from trafficking fund other nefarious activities such as organised crime and terrorism; and (3) human trafficking represents a particularly unacceptable failure of governance and social management.

As with other criminal activities, poverty is a driving force behind human trafficking. As Shankar Pratap Singh, former Deputy Inspector General of Police, Central Bureau of Investigation, has written, illiterate, innocent, impoverished, and hopeless "persons from underdeveloped and developing countries, in their urge to earn more money from overseas employment, fall easy prey to unscrupulous and unauthorized agents" of human smuggling.[54]

India is simultaneously a source, destination point, transit point, and aggregate domestic economy for human trafficking. Human trafficking is an extremely lucrative industry. In some areas, organised crime syndicates and other nefarious organisations control the industry directly. Elsewhere, trafficking enterprises are facilitated by networks of smaller organisations specialising in specific tasks such as enrollment, transportation, advertising, and selling.[55]

Organised Crime Syndicates

It is difficult to define organised crime precisely and comprehensively, but it can be broadly taken to mean "the unlawful activities of the members of a highly organized, disciplined association engaged in supplying illegal goods and services. Its essence is continuing illegal activities for generating illegal profits, the collective result of the commitment, knowledge and actions of three components—criminal groups, the protectors and specialist supporters" towards the goal of power and profit.[56]

Organised crime serves as the nexus between profit, an expansive human structure and often ideology, generally organised in hybrid networks in which a leader or 'Don' heads a highly distributed, adaptive, and resilient network of networks. Organised crime provides the glue that binds various crimes and pernicious and even licit networks on various scales.

Syndicates once based in single neighbourhoods of single cities and financed by single nefarious source[57] have extended their geographic and jurisdictional reach. Overlapping jurisdictions enable syndicates to engage in activities such as

> ...extortions, kidnappings for ransom, gun running, illicit trafficking in women and children, narcotics trade, money laundering using the *hawala* network, [smuggling, counterfeiting,] every conceivable kind of cheating and fraud, bank scams and so on, not only spread a sense of insecurity in the common man but also drain the country of organized criminal activity.[58]

Criminal networks have been extending to unforeseen geographic areas in recent years, and will continue to do so. Linkages between Mumbai, the United Arab Emirates (UAE), Karachi, Lahore, Kuala Lampur and several other places have facilitated local operations. Operations themselves have expanded into the financing of the movie industry, economic warfare on behalf of other governments[59] and terrorism.[60]

The expansion of these networks beyond the region, in cooperation with local groups in Asia, Europe, the Middle East, Africa, Latin America, and North America, is all too likely a possibility and would do a great deal to empower the capacity of criminal Indian networks.[61] Moreover, various licit and illicit industries—in the fields of transport, communications, outsourcing, natural resources; and in the emerging areas, such as electronic finance and nanotechnology—are vulnerable to organised criminal infiltration, manipulation and control.

The Trans-national Dimensions

The *Indian Diaspora* has reached sizeable populations in key regions such as East Africa, Southeast Asia, the Persian Gulf countries, and, in particular, the United Kingdom (UK) and the United States (US). The Diaspora has been seminal in bringing about a sea-change in India's global political and economic status. Remittances from the Indian Diaspora, including those from the Gulf, have given a boost to many economic sectors.[62]

Politically and strategically, lobbying by newly organised Indian Americans initiated trilateral economic and strategic ties with Israel and the United States, played a central role in inaugurating and managing the US-India nuclear cooperation deal that was ratified in 2008 and helped to usher in the broad based reassessment of US-India cooperation that may define the tenor of that emerging partnership.[63]

However, these benefits come with strategic costs for India's security. Many in the Indian Diaspora have provided funding for radical organisations that promote violence throughout South Asia. The Vishwa Hindu Parishad has a great deal of support from US- and UK-based Hindus who have provided political and economic support for many militant activities[64]; the Tamil Diaspora, particularly in the United Kingdom and Canada, has been seminal in supporting the LTTE in Sri Lanka financially, politically and diplomatically from their countries of residence[65]; hardline members of the Sikh Diaspora in the UK have kept the Khalistan movement alive[66]; and Islamic organisations and individuals throughout the world have transferred millions of dollars to Islamist terrorist organisations in Pakistan, Afghanistan and India, often by using charity organisations as fronts or covers for violent activities, though often inadvertently.[67]

In addition to funding crime, Diaspora groups can also provide political and logistical support for domestic actors. Lobbying by members of the Indian Diaspora in the US for example, has in the past swayed American political opinion in support of the Khalistan movement.[68] Both Diasporas and refugees that are sympathetic to a domestic cause can provide logistical support and safe-havens.[69]

Trans-national networks based on industries or supply of goods have turned India into a mere conduit for criminal activities that plague the whole world. Human, arms, and drugs trafficking, albeit of immeasurable harm to India, find both supply and demand in the rest of the world. Thus, a global perspective on all the local networks that affect India is essential for a more comprehensive understanding of the challenge.

Foreign governments such as Pakistan and China have long played central roles in India's domestic affairs as part of their strategic practices. A large number of the internal conflicts in India—the insurgency in Kashmir, the 1993 Mumbai bomb-blasts carried out by Dawood Ibrahim's 'D-Company' organised crime syndicate, conflicts in the northeast, and radical Islamist organisation—have been supported, strengthened and perhaps even maintained by external sources, particularly the Pakistani military and ISI. This interference has long been understood in India as the Pakistani military's endeavour to bring about India's "death by a thousand cuts" — a central issue in Indo-Pakistan relations.

A total end to the interference by external hands in domestic politics and conflict[70] is nearly impossible without resorting to means that would compromise India's integrity and democratic mandate, such as martial rule and sealed borders – both of which would be economically and socially unviable.

But it must be recognised that while many internal threats are supported and bolstered by outside sources, the roots of the problems — the initial impetuses –have almost always been local and internal, only to be exploited later by foreign elements. Moreover, so long as India is not in perfect harmony with every world actor— a highly unlikely scenario—external adversaries will seek strategic depth by interfering in India's domestic affairs. The space of opportunity for manipulation and the environment that enables such manipulation internally must be minimised, if not eliminated.

Simultaneously, as threats become increasingly trans-national in nature, and beyond the realm of Indian jurisdiction, closer coordination with other governments and jurisdictions will become necessary. At the micro-level, even domestic security can become a function of foreign policy.

Nexus

Each of the above-mentioned networked threats is individually a substantial security threat in itself. But what is truly ominous is the challenge posed by their nexus. Collusion and coordination among individual networks for tactical and strategic purposes is already widespread.

This is particularly true in India, where the lines between legal and illegal activities, organisations and persons involved are blurred in nearly every walk of life. Organised crime, for example, has linked up with local economic networks for money laundering and extortion, as well as with external intelligence networks, terrorist organisations, those controlling money and goods from narcotics, human and weapons trafficking, and instigators of communal conflicts.

An explosion of these long-distance, *weak ties* grants access to more information, resources, and influence across distances. What was once local is increasingly becoming global and these weak ties allow small changes to have large effects across the world.

The Threat of Governance

Personnel Retention and Morale

The opening of markets has made military and government recruitment economically less attractive than the private sector. Accordingly, the long-term prospects for sustaining government enrollment are diminishing.[71] Such a personnel deficit would seriously compromise the effectiveness of the military and security forces.

India's traditional military recruitment methods—namely from "martial races"—are currently failing, given changes in joint-family systems, migration, and other demographic shifts.[72] These demographic and market-driven effects on an insufficiently *large* talent pool are exacerbated by heightened demands of individual recruits. Military operations of the future will require a greater individual cognitive capacity, due to increased battlefield complexity.[73] As Major General Satbir Singh argues, "Future officers will need to be effective combatants, efficient administrators, proficient military managers and specialized military technologists."[74]

A talent pool that generates a sufficient number of recruits with adequate physical and mental capacities is required for the officer corps to face the increasingly complex external and internal security challenges. Such a talent pool is difficult to generate due to a lack of adequate educational facilities. As *The Economist* magazine writes, there is only a "privileged minority of college-leavers" among India's population that can pass the army's entrance exams to enter its officer corps.[75]

Privatisation and Accountability

In the past decades, outsourcing and privatisation of government services, processes and activities have been on the rise the world over. This has certainly been the case in India since the 1990s' liberalisation of the economy. Those in favour of privatisation[76] and disinvestment[77] cite its benefits as: increasing efficiency, transparency, competitiveness, growth, and decreasing the inertia in government processes.[78]

Many of these promises have indeed been realised and service provision has (with key exceptions) become far more effective and goal oriented. However, two key concerns that arise in the wake of the rise in power of markets are accountability and control over the use of force.

There have been a few high-profile cases in which private outsourcing companies have experienced information security breaches: namely, employees have sold clients' personal information for a fee to third parties and fraud of various sorts has occurred, though on a relatively low scale.[79]

Considering the greater level of privatisation of government processes—in part with the intent of eliminating the costs of in-house accountability measures—the accountability of the companies to which services are outsourced, as well as the security of information itself are serious concerns for the government.

Moreover, with the increasing cost and complexity of law enforcement and security operations, there has been a rise in the privatisation of security. India has not been immune from this trend. As Shantanu Chakrabarti has written:

> Village Defense Committees (VDCs), numbering nearly 3,700, have been put in place to encourage and equip the village community for self-defense against the menace of terrorism and supplement the ongoing efforts of the Security Forces. In addition, a large number of Special Police Officers (SPOs), numbering around 30,000, have been appointed. The Indian state has also used various vigilante groups in conflict zones.[80]

This trend will continue not only in *government* security processes, but also for private security purposes. The demand by companies and other clients for private security has increased the number of such firms. Modern-day 'mercenaries' of sorts—agents whose use of force threatens the traditional state monopoly – have also emerged; there are few international or domestic legal norms or statutes to ensure their accountability.[81]

As the United States and other Western countries have discovered,[82] Private Security Firms (PSFs) are a double-edged sword. On the one hand, they increase economic and political efficiency of security operations. On the other, since the private firms perform their task relatively free of external scrutiny, the important issue of accountability gets sidelined —a grave lacunae when dealing with a military or security force, whose actions could have a negative effect on public perceptions.[83]

If the lack of accountability becomes extreme, PSFs can be employed by corporations and other non-national actors for nefarious military purposes, or can add a political dimension to what is otherwise an exclusively military function.[84]

Systemic Enablers of Corruption and Mismanagement

Systemic enablers of corruption (the misuse of entrusted public power for private gain) and mismanagement (systemic inefficiencies in elements of the prescribed system) in the Indian governance system can precipitate massive security breaches and concomitantly enable threats.

Lack of faith in the Indian governance system and doubts about its efficacy in meting out justice may compel individuals and groups to seek the services of non-governmental, potentially nefarious sources of authority. Suketu Mehta cites a 1999 case in which even a senior judge in Mumbai sought the assistance of the underworld to recover a debt.[85]

Excessively repressive measures by government forces can compel pernicious organisation and non-state actors to resort to harsh reprisals. The insurgency in Kashmir is a powerful demonstration of such a backlash to abuses by Indian security forces.[86] The same can be said of the unending conflict situations in regions like Nagaland and Manipur.[87] Excessive repression—whether aberrations or norms—can detract from otherwise effective governance or counter-insurgency strategies. In Kashmir, for example, the Indian government's economic, social development and security provision work lost all significance in the Kashmiri mind because of the security forces' excessive violations of human rights with ostensible impunity. Any effort to effectively and peacefully govern Kashmir was irreversibly compromised.

After any bomb blast, the practice of many police forces is to resort to blind mass arrests of the so-called suspects (mostly the poor in Naxal-affected states or Muslims in urban areas) with the excuse of responding firmly to terrorism. Such arbitrary actions have served no purpose but to alienate the poor and the members of the minority community, further intensifying inter-communal tensions. That there is usually no such police response to Hindu perpetrators of violence adds salt to the wounds and has a threat-multiplying effect.[88]

Inherent in the corruption among government servants is the inevitable abetment of crime. The complicity of police forces in communal violence is an oft-cited example[89] in which politicised government servants support conflicts and crime. In 1993, the Mumbai police directly participated in the post-blast communal riots, in which over 1,000 people were killed.[90] There have been many other instances in which public officials have directly or indirectly colluded with, or sought the services of, organised crime outfits. In fact, many have cited corruption in government services and politics as *the key* enabler of organised crime.[91]

A telling example of inefficient management, particularly in the security sector, is a bureaucratic structure that does not match the level of complexity of today's scenario.[92] A organisation based on hierarchy cannot deal with a highly decentralised and networked threat because of the incompatibility between the threat and the selected response.[93] Likewise, a highly localised, decentralised response mechanism (such as a police force) may not be able to successfully contend with a large-scale threat (such as a conventional military force).

A prime example of incompatibility is the lack of lateral intelligence sharing across jurisdictions i.e. a hierarchical bureaucracy in dealing with networked information. After incidents such as terrorist attacks, very often, officials will come out with claims that there had been actionable intelligence regarding the incident, but that there was a communication gap or that the jurisdictions concerned did not act upon the given intelligence.[94] An excessively hierarchical response mechanism is incongruent with the increased rate, complexity, and networking of threats such as terrorism. Terrorist groups can communicate rapidly through networks, while law enforcement and intelligence agencies often fumble through the inertia of hierarchical bureaucracies. This incongruence *enables* threats to materialise.

Expectations and Realities of a 'Flailing' State

With a large and growing economy, strong electoral democracy, and relatively cohesive polity, it is difficult to argue that India is a failed or even failing state. Some, however, have aptly described India as a "*flailing* state," in which the head (policies, plans, laws, commissions, government apparatuses, etc) works appropriately, but the body and limbs (institutions, governance, bureaucracy, work culture, and *process* of implementing the mandates of the head) are either paralysed or flailing.[95]

India is rich in well-formulated, brilliantly planned commissions, laws, legal mandates, policies, and government apparatuses that aim to serve the cause of justice and to ensure social stability through effective governance. But the *processes of governance* remain highly questionable. What should be done is well understood, but *how* it should be done is a question that has remained unasked.

Many have experienced, commented on, and documented the corruption, cronyism, mismanagement, inefficiency, and lack of competence and work ethic that have become institutionalised in many of India's public service institutions.[96] This paradox of flailing gover*nance* despite the relative success of government is a phenomenon that needs to be examined.[97]

The most prominent security implication of this government-governance schism is on policy-making and execution. Vast discrepancy between the expectations of policy-makers and the on the ground results of policy execution is an unhealthy reality for a republic. If the government and the its leaders are under the impression that a threat has been dealt with through policy, but the matter remains unresolved due to ineffective policy execution, then the threat leaves the strategic radar while the leaders sit smug in blissful ignorance. Ultimately, when the unaddressed threat materialises, policy-makers are caught off guard. Such an imbalance between threats, perceptions, policy inputs, and policy execution (i.e. governance outputs) leads to otherwise avoidable strategic surprise.

Driven by other inefficiencies, mismanagement, and corruption,[98] this incongruence can cause massive harm to governance and society, including the danger mentioned earlier of disillusioned people seeking justice through alternate providers of services, as also the fragmentation of social spheres. India's efforts to address poor governance and bureaucracy have thus far been either too top-down (reform policies that have minimal effect at the micro-level) or too grassroots (NGOs that have minimal large scale effects). If there is to be any progress on social or security fronts, there is need to understand and infuse far greater efficiency in the processes of governance

The weakness of domestic governance has implications for economic growth and ultimately foreign policy as well. Gurcharan Das has written that India's economic success thus far has occurred "despite the state" rather than because of it, and has gone on to add that "China's leaders fear the day when India's government will get its act together." [99]

Macro Level Challenges

Indian's place in the world will be defined by two primary structural developments: (1) the empowerment of non-state actors; and (2) India's role as a rising power.

The same technologies and structural changes that have empowered sub-national actors on the micro level have empowered non-state actors in the international system. Increasingly, corporations, Diasporas, clandestine organisations, Civil Society Organisations (CSOs), activist groups, and other agents that are not bound by conventional notions of sovereignty, are having a profound effect on international affairs. Political or military relations between countries, including India, have often been initiated by engagement between private sector organisations and subsequently followed up by government contacts. This empowerment of non-state actors comes with many benefits, as they can serve as instruments of state policy or strategy, as well as with negative consequences, as it can sometimes come in direct opposition to the state's international aims.

As for India's specific role, much has been said about its 'rise to global prominence'. This is understandable because, with a recurring annual rate of economic growth of 9 percent, India is projected to become the world's third largest economy by 2030 and subsequently surpass that rank.[100] Indian global economic engagement and trade culture has increased steadily since the early 1990s, when India's economy opened up to foreign trade. There is little doubt that the nation will continue to grow in strength and gain international clout, as it is slowly, and cautiously, extending its reach into countries in Africa, Latin America, and Southeast Asia. Of course, this expected growth will bring in its wake far-reaching changes, one among them being expanded strategic and political horizons that can pose threats of greater magnitude. The challenges concomitant to such growth are manifold, and the nation needs to prepare for them.

How India engages with the world is up to India alone: on the verge of great power status, India cannot sit on its laurels. India must take advantage of, and *create,* opportunities while managing a great deal of challenges that will no longer come from point-sources.

Perception at the Macro Level

In the Age of Information, perceptions among states are gaining even greater prominence. Security concerns at the inter-state level are largely based on *perceptions*. Often, policies are formulated, weapons acquired and militaries formed to deter a hostile state or group from an act of offence rather than with the intention of offensive use. *Deterrence*, raising the adversary's perceived costs of an action in order to prevent its execution, is fundamentally an instrument of perception management.

At the state-to-state level, security can be taken to mean the incongruence between a threat posed (the *perceived* intentions and projected capabilities of an adversary) and the challenged state's ability to manage that threat (one's own response capabilities).

The *security dilemma* is a situation in which two or more states are drawn into conflict over perceived security concerns, though none of the states actually desires conflict. In such a situation, any step that one state takes to increase its security will cause the other to take an equal or greater step (given resource or political constraints), thereby decreasing the other state's relative security.[101] Though the 'security dilemma' has recurred over centuries, it takes on new angles with new sources of information, new modes of information transmission, and new centres of power. State policies articulated by government spokespersons are often belied by actions of official state apparatuses (clandestine agents, and different levels of state management, particularly in federalised systems), various media sources, as well as non-state actors within a country. Conversely, information about countries' capabilities, perceptions, and intentions has now become more transparent through the proliferation of information gathering systems.

At the global level, institutionalised perceptions tend to create paradigms that become the framework for that era's system of international affairs. From the end of World War II until the demise of the Soviet Union, the "Cold War" paradigm, in which countries were divided into either pro-Soviet or pro-American camps, framed the way that most countries behaved and were treated (the attempted 'non-aligned movement' notwithstanding). Likewise, the September 11, 2001 attacks in the United States brought about a 'paradigm shift' in international relations with the so-called "War on Terror"—and its echo, the "Clash of Civilizations"[102]—in which state relations were strongly influenced by perceived stances on terrorism, the very definition of which came with political overtones. These 'paradigms' have been largely forged by the articulated perceptions of the superpowers and thereafter imposed upon and adopted by other states for reasons of power dialectics, strategy, and political gains.[103]

Perception Management in the State System

Scholars of international relations often lay the blame for an outbreak of conflict on deficits or failures of communication and stress the need for states to make intentions more transparent. Confidence-Building Measures (CBMs) and diplomacy between states have been thought of as solutions to the problem. However, the fragmentation of global politics and the decentralisation of power in almost all governance systems have been so pervasive that even central governments exert less control over the actions of agents within their borders, thus allowing the actions to affect the perceptions in other states. For example, the Pakistan government claims that Pakistan-based militants who cross over into India are beyond their control, while India refutes this claim.[104]

Global *power projection* can be a tool of international *perception management*. Economic tools such as development aid and international investment are elements of power projection. Political devices such as facilitating peace negotiations, diplomatic intervention and non-offensive military activities such as humanitarian interventions, military training and exercises and even spending on military affairs and displays of military might are important modes of perception management in the international arena.

Depending on the direction India's strategy takes, it may seek to carve out its own global niche through its own means, circumventing conventional protocols. Indeed, India's own rise has been marked by economic factors—particularly information technology—and the country has been shaping an extended foreign policy through tools related to these factors. Relations with African countries[105] as well as those of the Middle East and Central Asia[106] have been largely shaped by technology-based development.

Soft power, the ability to influence the behaviour of other political entities through cultural or ideological means, is a central mode of international perception management. For centuries, India's soft power has been one of its greatest assets. It has long been argued that while India has never militarily invaded any country, it has 'conquered' much of Asia through the cultural influences of Hinduism and more profoundly, Buddhism. In the current era, Indian cuisine, brought by widely dispersed and well-established Indian Diasporas, Hindi films, Diasporas themselves, and other cultural facets have provided immensely powerful soft power influence for India throughout the world on both popular and governmental levels.[107] Such soft power also paves the way for smoother governmental contacts in the economic, political and strategic realms.[108]

State Perceptions: Pakistan

Regarding India-Pakistan relations, long seen within South Asia and without as the key and perennial international issue for the region, the enmity stems from a number of factors.

Many have discussed the power structures between the two countries that give rise to geopolitical "balances of power".[109] India, as a geographically proximate, physically larger country with a greater population, larger economy, and military and defence industrial base, clearly has the edge in the the power equation. The four factors that compel a state—in this case Pakistan—to perceive a more powerful principle as a *threat* are, according to Stephen Walt, aggregate power, geographic proximity, offensive power and aggressive intention.[110] By virtue of simple geopolitical structures, the first three criteria are satisfied in India's case, making it an "aggressive threat" in realist terms. The question of *why* either would necessarily have 'aggressive intensions,' however, remains explicitly unresolved in this schema.[111]

According to realist theory,[112] smaller, less powerful states have two options in dealing with a perceived aggressor: (1) they can balance against the aggressor, using their own, generally offensive capacities (internal balancing) or by joining other like-minded states against the aggressor (external balancing); or (2) they can bandwagon with the aggressor, "primarily to avoid becoming a victim, but sometimes also to share in the spoils."[113]

As Rajesh Rajagopalan explains,[114] Pakistan, as a less powerful state, would otherwise prefer to bandwagon, but is more inclined to balance against India because (a) Pakistan's is bigger than the other neighbours of India; (b) its extra-regional ties are enabled by a geography more conducive to extra-regional balancing than that of Nepal, Bangladesh or Bhutan; and (c) Pakistan, above all, perceives a powerful '*need to maintain its autonomy.*'

The 'aggressive intentions' exhibited by both the states, Pakistan's 'need to maintain its autonomy' and, in turn, enmity stemming from Pakistan's vehement resistance to 'bandwagoning' with an ostensibly aggressive India all emanate from various understandings of the two states' foundational ethos.

The very 'idea' of Pakistan has been unclear and undefined right from its inception, beyond fairly romantic and intentionally ambiguous notions of a 'nation for South Asia's Muslims'. This lack of clarity has frustrated all attempts to establish the nation's identity as well as to forge a viable system of managing a cohesive state.[115]

A lack of socio-political unity has resulted in two forms of intertwined militarism in Pakistan: internal and external. Internally, domestic division and fragmentation between the various ideological, regional, and ethnic factions of the country paved the way for military rule to forge national unity soon after independence.[116] Military control over civilian decision-making as well as the economy soon gave rise to a military-economic complex in which economic development, political management, and military rule became inextricable and mutually reinforcing.[117]

As Pakistani scholar Hussain Haqqani has written, this relationship has been reinforced by "the armed forces, [who] rationalize their dominant role by depicting India as an eternal threat to Pakistan's very existence. Given the military's power and its disposition to intervene in politics, civilian leaders cannot realistically pursue a path of accommodation with India or reassign national resources to development."[118] This military stance is reinforced by a much propagated view in Pakistan that its adversary, India, is not only a much bigger country with greater military capacities, but also that India "[denies] the very existence of Pakistan and would see to the destruction of Pakistan if it could."[119]

If enmity with India is a part and parcel of the Pakistani identity, then its traumatic dismemberment in the 1971 War against India could only have pushed this animosity deeper into the nation's mind. More than a political or military defeat, the severance of East Pakistan (now Bangladesh) from Pakistan was also a defeat to the foundational idea of Pakistan as a homeland for South Asia's Muslims. The loss strengthened the perceived notion that India rejects the idea of Pakistan and seeks its demise.[120]

Lacking a viable, coherent identity and humiliated by the defeat, it was inevitable that vengeful militancy take hold of the Pakistani military after 1971. The prominence of Kashmir in the Pakistani narrative, for example, increased for three main reasons: (1) as an external rallying point for domestic cohesion even in the wake of poor internal governance; (2) as a method of divesting India of a Muslim-majority province, thus, disproving the idea of India as a secular country and adding credence to its own 'two-nation theory'; and (3) exacting perceived justice on India for divesting Pakistan of its eastern wing.

In the last several decades, the military has supported sub-national militant Islamist organisations, within and outside Pakistan, to serve as strategic assets against India.[121] These organisations carry out terrorist attacks within Indian-administered Kashmir, Afghanistan and increasingly, across the rest of India. These groups give Pakistan an asymmetric upper hand over India, manipulating various weaknesses in Indian governance, while Pakistan itself has to do little on its own to reap the strategic benefits. These groups are in many ways Pakistan's most efficient and effective strategic weapons against India.

However, in a boomerang effect, the fallout of cultivating these groups has been the extension of the societal reach and power of these Islamist forces within Pakistan itself, such as the Taliban and its affiliates in the Northwestern Frontier Province (NWFP) and Baluchistan; and the Lashkar-e-Tayyeba (LeT) and Jamaat-ud-Dawa (JuD) in Pakistani-administered Kashmir, Pakistani Punjab, and Sindh.[122] These organisations have not only reinforced militarism against India, but have also extended the influence of their ideologies within Pakistan itself. Should this trend continue, Islamist extremist groups that were intended as mere tools of the Pakistani military may engulf Pakistan's society and the state itself, further reinforcing both internal and external militarism.[123]

Given the void in its own identity and the existence of a perceived 'permanent enemy,' Pakistan—and a domestic system that reinforces military rule and militarism—often identifies itself *against* India, and its own goals against India's success, rather than seeking a viable status of its own accord.

India fuels this division by indulging in the same fallacious bifurcation: Pakistan is often thought to be the single point-source of every threat.

First, this excessive focus on Pakistani malevolence—or some might argue, a lack of acquiescence[124]—"[appears] to validate the arguments of the more aggressive elements in the Pakistani military establishment" who hold that India seeks Pakistan's destruction, "thus fuel[ing] the unending conflict."[125]

Second, while perhaps grounded in legitimate concerns, the view that Pakistan is the single source of all threats allows India to ignore its internal problems, thus, allowing many threats to materialise. India tends to blame Pakistan for its own domestic weaknesses—in governance, state capacity, economic development and social tensions, all of which lead to conflicts. Whereas, more often, Pakistan only later manipulates problems that already exist in India.

Lastly, viewing the world through the bifurcated Pakistani prism holds India back in expanding its own international engagement. For a supposedly 'rising global power,' India's strategic vision is markedly narrow, focussing predominantly on the Indian subcontinent. As George Tanham writes,

> Delhi's nationalist elite believes that the subcontinent comprises one strategic unit, which is defined by geography and culture. Pakistan, Nepal, Bhutan, Bangladesh, and Sri Lanka are seen as basically of Indian culture…India's top strategic priority is its own stability and security, which is, at the same time, part of the subcontinent's: they cannot be separated...After World War II, the smaller units of the subcontinent… all became independent sovereign states, further breaking the unity of the subcontinent…Although India has outwardly accepted political reality in its declared policies, it often acts as if the old unity persists…India insists that it is not a threat to its neighbors, that it does not want to be, and that it cannot be because its neighbors' security is part of its own. Although the neighbors do not agree with this view, there is no truly sovereign state on the borders of India except Pakistan. Indians are offended by such observations and deny their validity.
>
> India's strategic aspiration is to serve as a friendly regional peacekeeper. It would like a Pax India to replace the earlier Pax Britannica. It sees itself as a benevolent nation and friendly policeman that seeks peace and stability for the entire region….Charges of being a bully are strongly rejected and resented by Indian strategists, although some of India's smaller neighbors see some of its actions in such terms. India not only hopes to play the role of peacekeeper but also that the role be acknowledged and endorsed by others, especially the great powers.
>
> Although most Indians accept Pakistan, some do not, and they still hold hopes that some day it will reunite with India in the old subcontinent.

This preoccupation with the subcontinent—and on Pakistan in particular— has kept India from seriously contemplating any global aspirations.[126]

For this and other reasons, military entanglements between Pakistan and India appear to be an inextricable element of the ideas of each nation-state's existence. And so, the perceptions of the other's malicious intentions are taken for granted.[127]

This fixation cannot be overcome unless at least one of the two primary drivers of the perception are altered:

- The state of Pakistan undergoes a domestic revolution in which its own identity and development are defined in ways that do not necessitate opposition to India. This would be aided tremendously by a dislodging of the military from civilian aspects of governance and, at the very least, a reconceptualisation of civil-military and 'military-mosque' relations in Pakistan.
- India seeks to alter the scale and realm of the relationship, namely by redefining its own vision of itself in the world and looking beyond South Asia as its sphere of influence and taking a broader, more proactive role in global governance. While bringing economic and strategic benefits for itself, such a redefinition would simultaneously quell the fear of India's neighbours (particularly Pakistan) that it is not in the business of subcontinental reunification. As the Mumbai-based Strategic Foresight Group has written, "if India is serious about a place at the [global] high table, Pakistan should not be an issue…India has wasted too much energy managing an adversarial relationship with Pakistan. If India wants to make a U-turn, it will only be possible with a new mindset and vision."[128]

State Perceptions: China

Bilateral ties between India and China have certainly thawed since their nadir during the Cold War. Expanded economic ties and joint military exercises have built confidence between the two countries. However, a primary concern of Indian diplomats and political analysts alike has been the asymmetry between the words and actions of the Chinese political elite.[129] Indeed, Beijing has sought to allay fears about its intentions by labelling its increased global prominence as a "peaceful rise," which itself was seen as too "confrontational" and changed to "peaceful development".[130]

Likewise, China's ability to project *soft power* is also of particular concern to many in India. China has established "Confucius Institutes" around the world in order to disseminate Chinese culture,[131] has purchased key media outlets in countries such as Nepal, and is involved in large-scale development projects in countries all over the Indian Ocean—most notably Pakistan.

China has cultivated strong relations with India's immediate South Asian Association for Regional Cooperation (SAARC) neighbours, the salient ones being:

- Bilateral ties with China account for 25 percent of **Myanmar's** total trade[132] and China is developing an oil pipeline through Myanmar to obtain direct transport access to the Bay of Bengal.[133]
- In **Bangladesh**, China has developed a container shipping facility at Chittagong.[134]
- **Pakistan** remains under China's economic and military umbrella, the latter having provided the former with nuclear technology ballistic missiles, aircraft, complete weapons systems[135] while China is currently developing a port at Gwadar, Pakistan, on the Arabian Sea.
- In **Nepal**, with the recent rise to power of Maoists, increased ties with the People's Republic of China (PRC) are anticipated through economic and military cooperation and perhaps even an extension of the Qinghai-Tibet railway from Lhasa to Kathmandu.[136]
- **Sri Lanka** has received Chinese assistance in the development of its Colombo and Hambantota Ports[137] and a weapons arrangement between the two countries involving the Chinese construction and weapons producer, Norinco[138]

It is feared that expanding Chinese influence—initially economic and perhaps thereafter military—in other South Asian countries such as Bhutan and Maldives, at present firmly in New Delhi's sphere of influence, will shift the regional balance of power out of India's hands.

Perception of China's malicious intentions and its emerging capacities has brought about the "String of Pearls" theory. As Christopher Pehrson of the US Army War College writes,

> The "String of Pearls" describes the manifestation of China's rising geopolitical influence through efforts to increase access to ports and airfields, develop special diplomatic relationships, and modernize military forces that extend from the South China Sea through the Strait of Malacca, across the Indian Ocean, and on to the Arabian Gulf. A question posed by the "String of Pearls" is the uncertainty of whether China's growing influence

is in accordance with Beijing's stated policy of "peaceful development," or if China one day will make a bid for regional primacy.[139]

However, whether China's "String of Pearls" should be perceived as a *security threat* to India is up to India alone. If China's capacities are thought to be harmful, then India can cultivate its own response capabilities to diminish the magnitude of the Chinese threat that is *perceived*. In other words, increasing India's ability to *manage* a potential challenge diminishes the level of the threat posed. This can be done by cultivating regional and global relationships of India's own that serve mutually beneficial political, economic and potentially military purposes.

State Perceptions: India's Smaller Neighbours

India's smaller neighbours' fear of Indian hegemony may also cause the latter to retreat from even positive engagements with India. Such a situation is anticipated with countries such as Nepal, which, in part out of economic need and in part out of fear of Indian control, is seeking engagement with China on economic and even political and military fronts.[140]

A key challenge for India is to create a balance between global power projection and regional aspirations. If India is to be a global power, it must extend its concerns globally and participate in the *definition* of the rules of international engagement. Such an extension would solidify the global emergence of India, as well as its *regional leadership*. India's international successes would also benefit its regional neighbours, rather than allowing it to be perceived as an antagonistic regional hegemon, which would make it an object of fear and hostility to its neighbours.[141]

State-to-State Conflict

Key deterrents to all-out conventional war in the modern age are inter-state linkages (economic, decentralised political ties, among others), power asymmetries, political backlash and fear of escalation. Indeed, while recent confrontations between India and Pakistan (Kargil in 1999) and the US-led invasion of Iraq represented state conflict, their low-intensity and predominant manifestation (i.e. insurgency), respectively, did not typify conventional war.

Asymmetries in power between India and its smaller neighbours have largely deterred or rendered unlikely conventional war (the last large-scale confrontation was the 1971 War with Pakistan, which resulted in dismemberment and an unconditional surrender for the latter). For this reason, India's adversaries have been forced to rely on asymmetric conflict such as proxy conflict, support for insurgencies, and far more decentralised modes of confrontation in seeking to counter Indian influence.

With regard to India's relations with Pakistan, imbalances in conventional weapons capacities favouring India have largely deterred Pakistan from pursuing conventional military strategies. This has driven Pakistan's military thinking towards two primary forms of unconventional conflict: (1) a first-use nuclear weapons policy to fend off any threat of escalation or even initiation of conventional conflict with India, which the latter would win; and (2) a reliance on asymmetric conflict that has taken a number of forms. These asymmetrical means include war by proxy (i.e. supporting elements hostile to India both within and outside India), offensive economic operations, interference and disruption of communications and infrastructure, etc. However, the occurrence of a hot conflict must not be ruled out. Contentions over Kashmir and incursions in that region, or the culmination of Pakistan-led asymmetric conflict (whether terrorism, insurgency, or otherwise) may lead to overt military confrontations between the two countries. The nuclear spectre over Indo-Pakistan relations adds both a degree of stability as well as heightened precariousness to the situation.

Despite increased cooperation with the PRC in the economic and military realms, tensions and rivalry will no doubt exist, given India and China's simultaneous global and regional emergence. A primary point of contention that may precipitate overt conflict would be the remaining border contentions in Aksai Chin and Shaksam Valley in Kashmir and Tawang in Arunachal Pradesh.

International Engagements in a New Global Order

In the past ten or fifteen years, India has extended the reach of its foreign policy far beyond its conventional realm, namely the subcontinent and

Indian Ocean. Economic relations have precipitated political engagements, and the trend is likely continue.

The Indian Ocean[142]

The end of World War II gave way to US hegemony over the Pacific Ocean region. The end of the Cold War brought a resolution to the Atlantic struggle. And now, many argue that the Indian Ocean will be "center stage for the Twenty-first Century."[143] The Indian Ocean comprises, as Robert D. Kaplan, articulates, "The entire arc of Islam, from the Sahara Desert to the Indonesian archipelago…global energy politics," as well as the key staging ground for "the rise of India and China." By virtue of geography, the Indian Ocean has long been India's 'backyard,' providing economic benefits, influence and security, as well as vulnerabilities.

Indian Ocean Area[144]

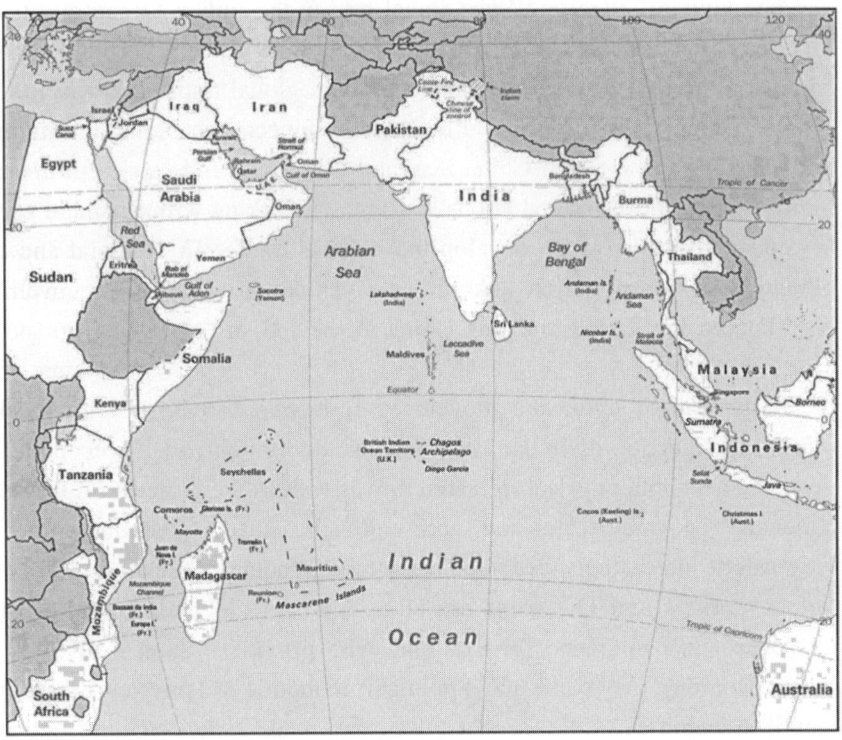

The Persian Gulf region sources nearly 66 percent and 35 percent, respectively, of the world's proven petroleum and natural gas reserves.[145] About 40 percent of petroleum products passes through the Strait of Hormuz, while 70 percent passes throughout the Indian Ocean (including the Gulf of Aden).[146] As Indian (and Chinese) energy consumption increases, access to, and the security of, these resources will be of increasing importance. Another area of focus in the ocean is sources of energy in African and Southeast Asian energy, especially coal in Mozambique and Australia and natural gas from Myanmar, Malaysia, and Indonesia.

As the comparatively new Caucasian and Central Asian energy markets mature, links between Azerbaijani, Kazakh, Uzbek, and Turkmen energy fields and the Arabian Sea will become ripe for development. (This is, of course, a medium to long-term prospect, contingent on the resolution of political-security impediments posed by the situations in Iran, Afghanistan and Pakistan).[147]

The Gulf of Aden and Suez Canal bridge the Indian Ocean and the Mediterranean Sea (and, thereafter, the Atlantic Ocean); accordingly, the bodies on the Red Sea are key chokepoints in global trade. Likewise, the Strait of Malacca is the primary body that connects the Indian Ocean to Southeast Asia, the South China Sea, and East Asia, and carries nearly a fourth of the world's traded goods.[148] China is working with Thailand and Myanmar, respectively, to develop the Isthmus of Kra in Thailand and a pipeline and transportation link across Myanmar in order to circumvent the Malacca bottleneck and link China to the Indian Ocean with greater ease.[149]

Expansion of trade and movement of labour also bring with them issues of protection of Indians and Indian interests abroad. As economic investments—both physical infrastructure as well as the presence of Indian nationals—become greater and more entrenched in other countries, their very safety increasingly becomes a matter of Indian national security.[150] Indian workers and Diasporas are also vulnerable in their countries of residence. Gulf migrants, for example, who provide a great deal to the Indian economy, may come under political, economic and physical attack in their host countries.

With the Indian Ocean gaining centrality in the global economy, the political and military implications of the body of water will surely follow suit. The potential for Chinese economic hubs—the 'pearls' in its string—to develop into military infrastructure cannot be ruled out. Likewise, the United States has recognised the Indian Ocean as a theatre of geostrategic importance and has been extending its own reach in the ocean. The entry of the United States adds another dimension to China's and India's engagement, compelling the latter two to seek alternative means of influence.

In his 1890 thesis on naval power, Admiral Alfred Thayer Mahan argued that the capacity to protect maritime commercial fleets had been the determining factor of power in world history, and that a robust naval capacity was necessary to project physical presence and ensure economic, and, thereafter, military strength.[151] With economic, political, and strategic interests in the Persian Gulf region, East Africa, Southeast Asia and Australia, India's position at the very centre of the emerging geopolitical playing field is both an asset and a liability.

The multi-Services' (Army, Navy, Air Force, and Coast Guard) command on the Andaman and Nicobar Islands extends India's ability to project power through Southeast Asia and the eastern Indian Ocean. This presence has already had strategic consequences. As Robert D. Kaplan has written:

> Zhang Ming, a Chinese naval analyst, has warned that the 244 islands that form India's Andaman and Nicobar archipelago could be used like a "metal chain" to block the western entrance to the Strait of Malacca, on which China so desperately depends. "India is perhaps China's most realistic strategic adversary," Zhang has written. "Once India commands the Indian Ocean, it will not be satisfied with its position and will continuously seek to extend its influence, and its eastward strategy will have a particular impact on China." These may sound like the words of a professional worrier from China's own theory class, but these worries are revealing: Beijing already considers New Delhi to be a major sea power.[152]

It should be noted that the Andaman-Nicobar base was expanded substantially under the Indian unified command in 2001, in the wake of a military review following the 1999 Kargil War.[153] But whether China's "String of Pearls" is a response to, or an impetus for, New Delhi's ostensible expansion is a point of contention between Indian and Chinese analysts. Former Indian High Commissioner to Pakistan G. Parthasarathy has written that "China has used such arguments to boost its naval presence in the Indian Ocean."[154]

India's politico-military influence in, and economic relations with, the Islamic world—most pointedly its development of the Chah Bahar port in Iran—may also be a point of power projection into the Indian Ocean's western reaches, enabling projection into the Persian Gulf, Western Arabian Sea, East Africa, as well as access to Central Asian energy and trade.

The tenor of potential conflict in the seas, however, is evolving and taking on new forms. In Southeast Asia, in addition to cross-border flows of arms, narcotics training for sub-national agents, maritime concerns stemming from strengthened SAARC and the Association of Southeast Asian Nations (ASEAN) are becoming prominent. Maritime challenges have taken sub-conventional forms, namely maritime terrorism and piracy that threaten the security of international maritime shipments throughout the Indian Ocean.

With intensified maritime trade comes the heightened relevance of port security. Maritime shipments throughout the world can be used for illegal transport of weapons, drugs, persons (both victims and perpetrators of crime) and even nuclear materials.

Though initiatives such as the Proliferation Security Initiative (PSI), the International Ship and Port Facility Code (ISPC), the Container Security Initiative (CSI), new technologies and information systems for heightened surveillance, and a degree of networked intelligence have emerged,[155] their level of implementation, breadth and effectiveness are questionable in India and other countries. Certain categories of threats are excessively intelligence-based and focus on nation-state cooperation, largely ignoring the highly decentralised, sub-national nature of the threats they pose.[156]

Tied to expanded trade is the security of Indian commercial and other long-distance modes of transport, such as ships, oil tankers and planes. In 2008 alone, the Indian Navy was involved in a number of sea-based military encounters with Somali pirates in the Gulf of Aden.[157] As these contacts expand, the security of sea-faring trade will gain greater importance and add another dimension to India's maritime security concerns. Policing and other measures to keep India's maritime routes and interests secure — both along its 7,516 km coastline[158] and further across the Indian Ocean—will be of central concern. Despite India's expanding naval capacities, other actors in the naval system may need to be engaged in multilateral security efforts. Such cooperation—whether with the United States, Australia, Japan, Middle Eastern and Southeast Asian nations, or even China—may also define the tenor of geostrategy in Asia.

Further Afield

Recently, India has begun to invest in energy and infrastructure projects in places as diverse as Africa, Latin America, Central Asia, the Middle East, and even Russia. Threats to these investments come from local sources as well as in transit (i.e. Indian investments can bear the brunt of political issues and weak governance in the countries of investment). The rise of piracy in the Gulf of Aden, an area governed only by ad hoc arrangements of the Western powers rather than by the region's states,[159] can directly harm Indian international economic and strategic interests. Likewise, in countries rife with rebel movements or civil wars, Indian investments could become the target, either as a deliberate political move against India's presence or just as part of the inevitable damage of any conflict, i.e., collateral damage.[160]

A key factor influencing India's future global economic (and thereafter political) engagements is the tenor of the emerging rounds of talks at the World Trade Organisation,[161] that are intended to frame the rights and responsibilities of countries vis-à-vis global markets. Depending on the outcome of the next round, India may be more open to external investment and will also have access to other, different markets in varying degrees of engagement.

If India becomes an increasingly strong political and military player in the world, its role in *international military coalitions* would become more pronounced. India has long been one of the main contributor of troops for international peacekeeping missions.[162] Such missions have become increasingly complex, and have the potential to bring troops themselves into the political arena of the conflicts they have come to contain. .

India has never sent its troops beyond its immediate neighbourhood, except under the auspices of the United Nations. But as India extends its political reach beyond its traditional regional jurisdiction, it may have to commit troops to new regions with different terrains and battlefield requirements. As India joins new multilateral institutions and security frameworks—a likely development—issues such as armed force interoperability and common defence planning become increasingly salient.

Nuclear Policy

India has long held an ostensibly paradoxical doctrine on nuclear weapons. While on the one hand, leaders like Jawaharlal Nehru and Rajiv Gandhi called for global nuclear disarmament,[163] on the other, India has continued to develop and maintain a "minimal credible deterrent" against nuclear threats, primarily from China and Pakistan. From the outset, India rejected the Nuclear Non-Proliferation Treaty (NPT) of 1970[164] on the grounds that it favoured the global nuclear status quo at the time—five nuclear "haves" that were coterminous with the permanent five members of the UN Security Council, and disadvantaged nuclear "have-nots," that is, the rest of the signatories. From 1974, when India tested its first "peaceful nuclear explosion," to 1998, India held an official position of "nuclear ambiguity." In that year, the ambiguity came to an end when India tested five nuclear devices in the Thar Desert of Rajasthan, to be followed suit almost immediately by Pakistan's test at the Chagai Hills of Baluchistan. These tests were followed as swiftly by US and Japanese sanctions against both countries.[165] By 2001, the sanctions were repealed, and in 2008 the US signed an agreement with India, ratified by the Nuclear Suppliers Group (NSG) that gives India access to commercially available nuclear technology, while mandating the separation of a number of civilian and military nuclear projects.[166]

Utility of Nuclear Weapons in an Age of Complexity

The global balance of power during the Cold War was often measured by the size and strength of a country's nuclear arsenal, namely those of the

United States and erstwhile Soviet Union. Since the Cold War's end, many new propositions regarding the 'currency of global politics' have emerged. Some argue that soft power is the key,[167] while Indian Prime Minister Manmohan Singh has argued that, in the light of India's software boom and the information technology revolution, *knowledge* will be the currency of world power in the 21st century.[168]

Nuclear deterrence—the *raison d'etre* of nuclear strategy—has been based on the concept of *Mutually Assured Destruction* (MAD). According to MAD, the use of nuclear weapons by two opposing sides would effectively result in the destruction of both the attacker and the defender, due to retaliation against the *known* aggressor. This situation works as a strong deterrent to initial use of the bomb. Accordingly, nuclear weapons were thought to have promoted stability by deterring even conventional conflicts between nuclear powers. But deterrence has not been foolproof, and has partly been disproved by the outbreak of two limited hot wars between nuclear powers—the border wars between the Soviet Union and People's Republic of China in 1969 and the Kargil War between India and Pakistan in 1999. Moreover, nuclear weapons have also encouraged greater reliance on proxy, low-intensity, and asymmetric warfare between nuclear weapons states—the Cold War between the United States and Soviet Union was essentially a global military conflict through proxies, while in South Asia, Pakistan has used the fear of nuclear escalation to expand its support for sub-national actors that threaten India.

Moreover, globalisation has so distributed power sources,that, unlike the case of US-Soviet, or even India-Pakistan rivalries, threats and enemies now do not necessarily come from single sources. In the current era of highly *decentralised* horizontal proliferation—including the A.Q. Khan's nuclear supply network, the unaccounted-for nuclear materials from the former Soviet Union and the potential collusion between state and non-state actors in the nuclear realm—the threats from nuclear materials no longer come from point-sources, against which retaliation would be possible.[169]

At the state to state level, many argue that nuclear weapons still play a central role. On one end of the political spectrum, Dr. Bharat Karnad has argued that nuclear weapons can and should be used as a key tool of power *projection*. In his book on *India's Nuclear Policy*, Karnad argues that India should assist Asian countries—namely Vietnam, Taiwan, and Japan—in developing nuclear weapons capacities in order to counter Sino-Pakistani nuclear cooperation and establish Indian hegemony in Asia, vis-à-vis China.[170]

Another leg of India's articulated nuclear posture—preceding even its development of a nuclear weapons capability—is global nuclear disarmament, a policy that India's political leadership has long espoused as a theoretical—though arguably not actionable—ideal. Indeed, it was this very profound imprint on Indian thinking that compelled post-Independence India to initially keep its hands clean of nuclear weapons and, following the 1974 tests, maintain a stance of nuclear ambiguity. As the Indian Ministry of Defence's Annual Report of 2001-2002 maintains:

> India remains a consistent proponent of general and complete disarmament and attaches the highest priority to global nuclear disarmament...The nuclear tests of May 1998 do not dilute India's commitment to this long-held objective...As a nuclear weapon state, India is even more conscious of its responsibility in this regard and, as in the past, initiatives in pursuit of global nuclear disarmament continue to be taken.[171]

However, given the extent to which nuclear weapons have proliferated, current global realities make Indian unilateral disarmament a highly unlikely prospect. As Ashley Tellis has written:

> [Pakistan's] overwhelming fear of India more than suffices to ward off the worst political pressures imaginable; Pakistan will risk internal stagnation and decay if necessary but will not exacerbate its external vulnerability by succumbing to any pressures for denuclearization as long as India, its archrival, refuses to move in a similar direction first. India...will refuse to contemplate any such step [towards denuclearization] as long as China, its principal long-range threat, remains a significant nuclear power—and China, it may be surmised, would decline to consider denuclearization as long as Russia and the United States, its strategic rivals, refuse to consider

> denuclearization themselves. Thanks to this long and extended chain of consequences, no movement toward denuclearization should be expected in South Asia within the policy-relevant future.[172]

This chain of nuclearisation has made any reversal of the status quo contingent on change in its strongest link, namely, the United States. And, as Robert Joseph and Ronald Lehman write in a report on *US Nuclear Policy in the 21st Century*, "The knowledge to build [nuclear weapons] will continue to exist; they cannot be disinvented." Thus, the *potential* need to respond to, or deter, a nuclear attack will remain. "Whether we like it or not, nuclear weapons will [likely] be part of the global security setting."[173]

Despite the presence of nuclear weapons in the global political calculus, their specific *role* for a country like India remains unresolved. With the end of the Cold War and the decline of state-to-state nuclear apprehensions, the *military utility* of nuclear weapons has in many ways diminished. And as General Ved Malik articulates, nuclear weapons "are not usable in a war. They make the war neither fightable nor winnable."[174]

It is with this in mind that India's doctrine of a Credible *Minimal* Deterrent (CMD) remains salient. CMD refers to the ability to deter a strike with one's own ability to cause *sufficiently devastating*, rather than massive, retaliatory damage. Indeed, India's strategic thinking has, for reasons of both resource constraints and ideology, favoured the political role of nuclear weapons—the deterrent to escalation and even initiation of conventional warfare—over their military usability.[175] Having deemphasised the military function of nuclear weapons, India has kept its arsenal non-weaponised (requiring assembly and placement on delivery platforms, thus, delaying response time) and under strict civilian control, a central element of India's nuclear doctrine.[176]

Nuclear 'Strategy'

Since the 1998 nuclearisation of the Indian subcontinent, India has espoused an overt doctrine of No-First-Use (NFU) and non-use against Non-Nuclear Weapon States (NNWS). Meanwhile, the most proximate nuclear threats pose diverse challenges: China affirms a similar doctrine of NFU and non-use against NNWS,[177] while Pakistan espouses a first-use policy to compensate for its conventional inferiority vis-à-vis India.

Contested borders with China—particularly in Arunachal Pradesh—are thought to be a flashpoint of Sino-Indian conflict, which may even tread into the nuclear realm. "India's strategy for dealing with a nuclear China today consists simply of [seeking to maintain] superior conventional capabilities along the contested border."[178] Should a conflict break out over the region, India's conventional superiority in the area would place the onus for nuclear escalation on China, a prospect that India believes would be avoided by India's nuclear deterrent.[179]

With Pakistan, Kashmir is thought to be a nuclear flashpoint. Many have argued, however, that the nuclear umbrella under which Indo-Pakistani relations have operated since 1998 has had harmful effects on bilateral relations. Because of the Pakistani first-use doctrine, Indian politicians fear that any sort of direct, even retaliatory conventional confrontation could quickly escalate to the nuclear level. Accordingly, Pakistan is thought to be able to carry out asymmetric warfare—i.e. supporting terrorists and insurgents—against India with relative impunity.[180]

Given the retaliatory capacity of both countries, deterrence is likely to hold.[181] Ashley Tellis articulates two key uncertainties that could lead to the failure of deterrence:

> The first uncertainty derives from the presence of weak state structures and, by implication, the possibility of deficient strategic decision-making, especially in Pakistan[182]... [The second uncertainty stems from the possibility of 'catalytic' wars], conflicts brought about either by the actions of third parties or by the principals involved with the intention of entrapping third parties into intervening in an ongoing conflict.[183]

As the strategic environment and other states' arsenals evolve, what is considered "minimum" in order to stay "credible" may change as well. Drivers of this evolution may include new types of weapons such as low-yield or other tactical nuclear weapons, nuclear-tipped missiles with increased payloads and ranges, as well as new doctrines in which nuclear weapons play alternative strategic roles.

The credibility of a nuclear deterrent is, as K. Subrahmanyam writes, not "based on mere numbers but on its survivability [to counter-force strikes]. Survivability ensures that no nuclear aggressor, however powerful, can be certain that his first strike would eliminate all the weapons of the opponent, and that the opponent's nuclear weapons will not get through and cause unacceptable damage to the aggressor."[184] Accordingly, the distribution of India's arsenal, in order to increase survivability and, in turn, deterrent credibility, is underway, with the development and deployment of "air, sea, and land forces" with missile capabilities.[185]

While force distribution may increase credibility, it would also raise India's arsenal status from a "recessed deterrent" to the status of a weaponised "ready arsenal."[186] While 'readying' India's arsenal may increase the credibility of the deterrent, it would also increase the credibility of the threat perceived by China and Pakistan, compelling the two to further develop and perhaps deploy nuclear weapons, setting off an Asian arms race.

As protection from surprise nuclear attacks, India is keen on developing its own Ballistic Missile Defence (BMD) capacity and, to that end, it is developing its land-based BMD such as the sensor-enabled Prithvi missile (which was recently given anti-ballistic capacities) to intercept ballistic missiles that may come from Pakistani or Chinese sources. The threat of Islamists taking over Pakistan's military, and, in turn, its nuclear forces, has engendered a strong perception of the need to possess the ability to instantly intercept offensive missiles of increasing ranges.

However, the viability of India's BMD, even in the long-term, is questionable. Whether the technology would be able to field an onslaught of missiles in the event of a full-scale attack, outside of controlled testing, remains unresolved. Given the geographic proximity of the Pakistani and Chinese arsenals (an issue exacerbated further given the burgeoning Chinese nuclear submarine development), the sufficiency of India's BMD response time and the possibility of false signals are central concerns. As Bharath Gopalaswamy writes:

> The estimated total missile flight times are 8-13 minutes for ranges of 600-2,000 kilometers [for Chinese and Pakistani weapons]. The flight times can be even less if the missile is flown in a depressed trajectory. Such a short time period places stringent conditions on procedures for evaluating and verifying warnings. There would be no time to consult or deliberate after receiving this warning. In other words, any response would have to be predetermined, presenting a significant likelihood of accidental nuclear war from false alarms.[187]

BMD technology acquisition comes with burdensome costs and strategic implications; obtaining the requisite technology would require strategic partnerships with Russia, Israel, and the United States, the only countries with anti-ballistic missile capacities. These concerns notwithstanding, BMD brings the potential to *escalate* the scale of nuclear weapons conflict. If land-based BMD gives way to sea and even *space-based* missile defence, a large-scale weaponisation of space and an arms race is sure to follow.

Space Policy

India is one of the few countries where a space programme developed predominantly from the civilian end and has only recently moved towards enabling military infrastructures. Even now, India's space-based programmes are largely restricted to civilian projects. The Chandrayaan-1 moon mission of 2008 is primarily for civilian purposes of information gathering, but paves the way for subsequent missions to Mars.[188] Position navigation systems such as Gagan and Indian Regional Navigational Satellite System (IRNSS) are also key projects of the Indian Space Research Organisation (ISRO).[189]

Civilian Development vs. Militarisation vs. Weaponisation

Satellites placed in space have powered civilian infrastructure such as mobile phones, the internet, and global navigation systems, providing a flexible backbone to telecommunications development. It has been through these technologies that developing countries like India have been able to 'leap-frog' into the space age by developing mobile communication networks, making obsolete cable-based telecommunications systems. Most recently,

India has developed a number of commercial satellites and launch vehicles, such as the Polar Satellite Launch Vehicle (PSLV), Geosynchronous Launch Vehicle (GSLV), and GSLV Mk III, which have been used for scientific research and for launching satellites for other countries.[190]

Similar space-based technologies and systems have also enabled military components of high-tech warfare, such as network-centric warfare and precision-guided missiles. While bandwidth availability remains an issue, communications, surveillance, intelligence gathering and guidance satellites for military purposes (without active weapons) have been supported by space-based systems. India does not have any satellites dedicated explicitly for military application, but dual-use technology has been a key component of its space strategy.

While space-based infrastructure has simultaneous civilian and military purposes, no state has weaponised space as yet (i.e. placed offensive weapons in space). While this seems unlikely in the near-future,some argue that it is inevitable, given the recent trends in military and strategic thinking, namely the "Revolution in Military Affairs" (RMA).[191] Indeed, there have been no quick moves to enact any international treaties or legal frameworks banning the deployment of weapons in space.[192]

Key developments that have hampered any international movement against the weaponisation of space are the recent US withdrawal from the Anti-Ballistic Missile (ABM) Treaty and its threat to deploy offensive military capabilities in space. The deployment of a space-based ballistic missile shield by any state, with the intention of downgrading the effectiveness of other countries' missiles would also be an impetus for global space engagement.

The Chinese Anti-Satellite (ASAT) test in January 2007 was also a turning point in the global space 'race.' Primarily, the action had contradicted China's previous stated policy, signifying that such incongruity, as well as offensive engagement in space, could be the shape of things to come. Moreover, the destruction of the satellite itself came with strategic implications of its own. First, it demonstrated China's ability to destroy satellites of all sorts—including those of other states. Second, the debris that resulted from the missile destruction, collision with which could harm any country's space assets, serves as a deterrent to further development of other countries' space assets, including those related to militarisation or weaponisation.[193]

Any act of space weaponisation is certain to start off an arms race. On the legal front, the treaty on the Prevention of an Arms Race in Outer Space (PAROS) was rejected by the US, which has also discussed the possibility of denying the use of space for other nations' intelligence gathering purposes. Also, there has been a trend against legal regimes that oppose such unilateralism.[194]

Civilian Capacities

Beyond the more manifest strategic imperatives of space-based technologies centring on militarisation and weaponisation, other civilian necessities—namely, *energy needs*—are central dimensions of space exploration, particularly for a developing country such as India.[195]

The launch of the research satellite Chandrayaan-1 in 2008 was primarily for the sake of collecting information about the moon's material composition. Data regarding the potential mineral resources, ice deposits, and other natural resources—oxygen, hydrogen, nitrogen, uranium, etc —was sought for future exploration and possible harvesting for energy purposes.[196] According to India's former President A. P. J. Abdul Kalam, India's moon missions will develop Indian research and resource extraction capacities, and serve as intermediary bases for future missions to Mars.[197]

Space-based solar panels (Solar Power Satellites — SPS) hold great potential for the future of energy harvesting and, in the long run, could prove to be the most cost-effective method of sourcing energy. Solar power satellites have the advantage of unfettered access to solar rays unaffected by daily or seasonal cycles or weather patterns, zero emissions after their initial deployment, and minimal waste.[198]

A key impediment to their development, however, is the extremely high initial investment, as well as the low return on the currently available absorption technology. These impediments will likely be diminished in the medium to long term by gap-bridging technological advances.

George Friedman of the policy group Stratfor, projects that space-based energy assets—particularly space-based solar power—will be a primary source of energy production in the future, and that their control will be a key determinant of global economic and military power.[199] India's current edge in the production and deployment of satellites may well carry over into strategic advantage in the development of SPS. However, the high costs of research and development into these and other space-based sources of energy may necessitate international cooperation in their development, which will come with broad strategic implications as well.

Any space-based infrastructure, military or otherwise, however, may be exposed to major vulnerabilities, including those that can outright destroy any space-based infrastructure. Such vulnerabilities include: anti-satellite systems, such as *lasers* that can reach space-based targets instantly and minimise debris; *ballistics*, such as the projectiles associated with missile defence that would have the ability to destroy infrastructure in space; collision (or *crashes)* with other space-based infrastructure; and most perniciously, *debris* caused by in-space explosions that could destroy placements in space through collisions.[200]

Technology and Information in Military Affairs

Network-Centric Warfare (NCW) began as a theoretical concept for US military transformation with its origins in the mid-1990s' strategic military planning and the broader RMA. NCW was devised with the goal of adapting 21st century warfare for an era of accelerating change and increasingly complex combat situations ushered in by the information and technological revolution of the 1990s. John Gartska and David Alberts describe NCW as:

> An information superiority-enabled concept of operations that generates increased combat power by networking [geographically dispersed] sensors, decision-makers, and shooters to achieve shared awareness, increased speed of command, higher tempo of operations, greater lethality, increased survivability, and a degree of self-synchronization. *In essence, NCW translates information superiority into combat power by effectively linking knowledgeable entities in the battlespace*[201]

Key aims of NCW are (a) to enable military commanders to cope with the increasing informational and sensory complexity of the battlefield; (b) to increase force agility and adaptability through rapid communication; and

(c) to enable the upper echelons of military command greater situational awareness; and increase integration among the Army, Navy, and Air Force.[202]

Certain elements of the Indian NCW policy—namely the empowerment of the *upper* echelons of command and large-scale integration—differ markedly from American net-centric military doctrine. The latter aims to flatten hierarchies by giving lower-levels of command greater operational and tactical flexibility, while enabling upper echelons a 'bigger-picture view' of the battlefield. The Indian doctrine, however, seeks to centralise all information, which means authority and decision-making powers will continue to be held by at the upper echelons of command.[203]

Fundamentally, net-centricity enables greater flexibility and agility of forces. In their book on net-centricity and future warfare, David Gompert, Irving Lachow and Justin Perkins argue that networking (1) enhances situational awareness due to the ability to collate and disseminate the products of a number of distributed, connected sensors; (2) enables greater *precision* in sensor and weapons effects, via weapon-guidance data and target-location and; (3) allows the *dispersal* of force elements while managing them as a concerted unit.[204]

Tied with network-centric warfare and information-driven operations is the military *hardware* that NCW enables. A revolutionary development comprises the *Precision-Guided Munitions* (PGMs), or "smart weapons". PGMs are weapons guided by computers and space-based infrastructure to strike selected targets from afar with great accuracy, minimising casualties, harm to civilians and fallouts from the blast.

In *The Future of War*, George Friedman and Meredith Friedman argue that "where guns and artillery are inherently inaccurate and need to be fired thousands of times to hit one target, [PGMs will be] precise and lethally efficient; while ballistic weapons platforms must be brought within range of the battlefield, PGMs can devastate from any distance." They go on to argue that these weapons will render obsolete the key hardware of military might—tanks, warplanes, and carrier groups.[205]

Network-centric warfare, information sharing and diffusion, as well as the information and guidance required for PGMs, are enabled by space-based platforms, which may take on an increasingly central role in military affairs, power projection, and inter-state and global conflict.

Net-centricity is not only an enabler of one's own operations, but as various countries and military forces[206] adopt network-centric tactical doctrines, the *deficit* of networked, agile, and flexible forces can become an opportunity cost, and bring about an asymmetry in capacities. As Gompert et al, articulate:

> If each of two opposing forces enjoys [the benefits of net-centricity], its ability to operate while dispersed could be offset by the other's ability to find, target, and destroy its forces with precision. The net effect, theoretically, is that *both* forces would be more vulnerable than if opposed by non-networked forces, though not necessarily equally vulnerable. Even the superior and better networked of the two forces would be more exposed—unless and until the inferior force was decimated—which could alter the costs and course of combat.[207]

The above-mentioned quote touches upon a central premise and implication of network-centric operations: *the role, accessibility and security of information itself.* Local information is transmitted and accumulated in order to bring about global knowledge and macro-awareness. However, if the quality of the transmitted information is poor—inaccurate or misleading due to error or intention as part of a disinformation campaign or security breach—the security of the resulting operation, and of the system as a whole, is compromised.

Likewise, the effectiveness of PGMs relies, in addition to the precision of the weapons themselves, on the accuracy of the information regarding the target. If the quality of information is poor, the operation suffers.

Emerging India and Strategic Culture

The global 'proactivity' of the Indian economy has, according to many, not been matched in the politico-strategic sector of Indian foreign policy formulation.[208] As General Ved Malik (Retd) has articulated, India's

> ...vast diversity has made us culturally a strong soft power with a global philosophy of *vasudhaiva kutumbakam*—the world is one large family. Most of our political leaders grew up conjuring the idea of a morally superior India; professing peace and harmony in a world where nations indulge in cut-throat competition. Value-based politics is morally superior. But...that does not reflect the international realism. The ability to generate hard power, and the will and ability to make use of that, is not our strong point.[209]

From this perspective, India's strategic culture has been largely reactive, rather than proactive. Through the course of India's history, India's leadership has published few comprehensive strategic documents, and long-term planning (beyond five-year economic plans) has been relegated in favour of more proximate thinking. Reactivity may come with many benefits, including a penchant for quick and effective *adaptation* to dynamic challenges and flexibility in the face of adversity.

However, some argue that the costs of such an approach outweigh the benefits. Dr. Bharat Karnad, for example, has argued that "the historical burden of Indian inaction post-1947, lack of strategic vision, initiative and proactive national security policies, when juxtaposed against China's growingly confident claims for its right of presence and role ...augurs ill for India's interests and prospects."[210]

The existing reactivity stems partly from the lack of a specified, articulated, and coherent global strategy of power acquisition and projection. India's primary strategic goals have, for the majority of its independent existence, focused on more proximate and short-term matters. As articulated by George Tanham in 1992, these key strategic goals—extracted from various documents, papers, actions, and statements over the decades rather than single cohesive articulations— included:

(1) The prevention of India's small neighbours from solicitation of external support deemed inimical to Indian interests;

(2) The development of capabilities to (a) deny Pakistan a meaningful potential to challenge Indian predominance on the subcontinent; and (b) deter or defeat hostile Pakistani actions;

(3) Obtain the resources to (a) fight a two-front war, thereby keeping any potential Chinese challenge at bay; and (b) achieve symbolic 'power equivalence' with China;
(4) Achieve close relations with the Soviet Union to counter China and Pakistan;
(5) Develop naval capabilities that (a) could deny any extra-regional power from achieving a meaningful naval presence in the Indian Ocean; and (b) would give India superiority over any combination of local navies, thereby seeking legitimacy for Indian predominance in the Indian Ocean; [and perhaps the most comprehensive of all],
(6) Approach world power status by developing nuclear and missile capabilities, a blue-water navy, and a military-industrial complex—the obvious characteristics of superpowers. Yet recognition as a *great world nation* (rather than as a super power) *was the paramount goal.*[211]

The tenets outlined by Tanham (particularly 1-4) speak of a strategy defined in short-term, regionally specific terms. A notion of 'Pax India,' in which India serves as the de facto peacekeeper and regional hegemon of South Asia is the only strategy that India articulates and acts upon.[212]

While it is a strategy that may have been relatively effective—and realised in most respects— it has simultaneously soured many of India's bilateral relations in the subcontinent.[213] Moreover, such a regional focus has been to the detriment of any planning in India's global ambitions, namely its "recognition as a Great *World* Nation."

As India's economic, political, and strategic presence around the globe becomes more prominent, thereby increasing and diversifying the challenges to its security, such a reactive, myopic strategy may quickly prove insufficient. Even the development of Indian great power status, as articulated by Tanham (number 6), is largely reactive. A check-list of military attributes of other 'great powers' is made and it becomes the goal to develop those attributes as well.

While the "currency of global politics" may certainly be defined by certain elements, in the light of the collapse of the Soviet Union and the bipolar world, what those elements are, is still under reconsideration.[214] The broader strategic environment will define certain tenets of that 'currency', but India needs to play its role as a credible global power by *contributing* to that strategic environment as well as to the *definition* of what makes a power 'great.'

Accordingly, India can take a far more active role in global governance, whether it be in: nuclear non-proliferation concerns as it moves towards becoming a *de jure* nuclear power;[215] conflict resolution, economic development and better governance in Africa; encouraging development and engagement with Latin America; encouraging a greater nexus between human and financial capital in the Middle East and Central Asia; and, contributing to the resolution of global and regional conflicts. As a country that serves as the bridge to a number of 'civilisations'—Dharmic, Islamic, Buddhist and East Asian, and Western and Liberal—as well as having a vast human capital stemming from education and technology development, India is particularly well suited to play such global roles.

As part of this proactivity, India should articulate an adaptive yet coherent National Strategy that would "articulate a vision of the current and future [strategic] environment, communicate [India's] values in the twenty-first century, develop a framework for collaboration across government on national security policy and identify policy areas where departments and agencies can be more efficient and effective in working together, and prioritise national security policies and initiatives and the allocation of resources."[216] A National Strategy would certainly not be an exact rendering of the future, but rather, articulate India's goals, aims, and vision of its own role in the world, and thereafter, shape the path towards their realisation.

Micro-Macro Interactions

Globalisation has empowered individuals and groups, as well as states in their respective domains. While these domains have been altered even when considered in isolation, the interaction between the 'state-centric' system and the 'multi-centric' systems[217] creates a third realm of micro-macro interactions that drive new sources and types of changes. Challenges become simultaneously global and local, and develop concurrently inside the realm of the state and in the realm of individuals.

For India, the emergence of micro-macro linkages takes on an increasingly meaningful role as India and its people engage with the world in unprecedented ways. The role that governments have in defining, creating and managing problems, and the role that individuals and groups have in creating, transmitting and resolving them become exceedingly complex as conventional barriers of space, time and jurisdiction are crossed with increasing ease. Moreover, the *interactions* themselves are self-reinforcing: individuals and groups shape states and their activities and macro structures such as the state[218] shape and often constrain the activities of individuals and groups.[219] However, the relationships of influence between agent and structure become increasingly reciprocal at a time when micro-level actors have started to gain power in global affairs.

Ultimately, it is complexity—the ever growing interconnectivity, interactivity and change on multiple levels of what are fundamentally multiple systems—that typifies trends and events on the level of micro-macro interactions. Due to their multi-scale, interactive nature, challenges are not easily compartmentalised into jurisdictions, scales, or disciplines.

Nuclear Security

The sub-national trafficking of nuclear materials has become a great threat since the fall of the Soviet Union. Arsenals in the former Soviet states of

Central Asia in particular—where the Soviet Union engaged in uranium mining, plutonium production, fabrication and testing of biological and chemical weapons, and storage and testing of nuclear weapons—have been extremely vulnerable to infiltration, tampering, and material theft by sub-national actors.

The material of these leftover arsenals can be classified into (a) nuclear weapon-related material, including fissile material (highly enriched uranium and plutonium) and radioactive material (often abandoned sources); (b) biological weapon-related materials and technologies; and (c) chemical weapon-related materials and technologies.[220] The security of these materials in the wake of the Soviet Union's collapse was at best tenuous. The US spearheaded the efforts to secure the materials. It launched the Nunn-Lugar Cooperative Threat Reduction (CTR) programme, which: consolidated the entire arsenal under Russian control; dismantled weapons of mass destruction; increased military counter-proliferation cooperation; and gave financial assistance to unemployed scientists with access to nuclear materials, so as to deter them from selling the materials on the black market.[221]

In its early years, the CTR was a great success, particularly in the transfer and reduction of weapons. However, it has, since the late 1990s, received minimal attention, and many loopholes in the security of Central Asian nuclear materials remain.[222] The prospect of these materials being sold on the black market to state and non-state actors—including terrorist groups—exists.[223]

To compound these threats of trans-national nuclear smuggling, nuclear proliferation networks run by Pakistani nuclear scientist Abdul Qadeer Khan were exposed in January 2004.[224] Since the late 1980s, Khan had run a nuclear materials supply network through countries as diverse as Libya, North Korea, Iran, Saudi Arabia, Malaysia, and elsewhere. The network's headquarters were in Dubai, and it was largely directed by Buhary Sayed Abu Tahir, a Sri Lankan living in the United Arab Emirates whose company, SMB Computers, served as a front for Khan's proliferation network.[225] The activity of the network stretched as far as West Africa, North Africa, Southeast Asia, Europe, North Korea, and further. The full extent of the network is still a mystery.[226]

The coupling of these nuclear supply networks with terrorist organisations and even adversarial, irresponsible, or irrational[227] states can bring about a catastrophic scenario in which a sub-national actor—to whom the accountability-ensuring doctrine of *Mutually Assured Destruction* does not apply—can possess, detonate, or threaten to detonate a nuclear weapon, or a Radioactive Dispersal Device (RDD), commonly known as a "dirty bomb."[228]

The security of India's own domestic nuclear materials and other targets is also an issue of major concern. Nuclear power plants, research reactors or other facilities and laboratories can be the target of theft, sabotage, and terrorist attacks—risks that apply to many of India's own facilities as well as those around the region.[229]

Till now, the control over nuclear materials and facilities has been under the fairly centralised, and, thus, relatively firm and accountable command of the Indian public sector, particularly the Department of Atomic Energy[230] But now, with the 2008 passage of the Indo-US Civilian Nuclear Deal, it may become far more decentralised, with other countries' governments and private sector firms playing increasingly greater roles in the development of India's nuclear programmes.

The role of these companies and other actors can certainly come with many benefits, economic, scientific, political, and strategic. But such an opening up of the nuclear industry can pose new challenges to accountability and the security of nuclear materials and information .[231]

Frontier Security

At no time since the emergence of the nation-state, have national and regional borders been so incapable of restricting the flow of information, finances, and goods. This is due to the information revolution and the opening up of markets that has a strong impact on a state's security. While political allegiances can shift and economic ties fluctuate, geography is a constant that defines the very meaning of a nation-state.

Political Issues

Outstanding border issues between China and India flared up into a war over Arunachal Pradesh and Aksai Chin in 1962. Tensions over the regions remain high between the two countries and, if unresolved, may lead to hot conflict as the roles of each sector in the political and economic development of both countries increase. Moreover, trafficking—particularly of arms and to a lesser degree, drugs—from China through India's northeast border has long been a matter of concern for India.

With Bangladesh, political, economic and environmental refugees pouring into India through a porous border have been the key strategic threat from that country. With Myanmar, trafficking—of drugs and weapons—is the main concern.

Migration from neighbouring states such as Bangladesh, Nepal, and Bhutan has already strained the capacities in India's north and northeast. Indeed, Bangladeshi refugees from the 1971 War into India's northeast provided the impetus for a resumption of a local conflict in the subsequent years. Recently, migration from those regions has provided the ground for the resurgence of the nativist and xenophobic movements of that region.

In addition to the backlash against the very presence of foreigners, illegal cross-border migration brings nefarious agents onto Indian soil. The porous borders between India and Bangladesh, for example, have enabled members of the United Liberation Front for Assam (ULFA) to train in Bangladesh and carry out attacks in India, and also serve as a conduit for the Bangladesh-based Harakat-ul-Jihad-ul-Islami (HuJI) and even Pakistan-based terrorists to enter and India.

Economics also plays a role in India's northeast borders. The Kunming Initiative of 1999 paved the way for economic relations between India, China, Myanmar, and Bangladesh through India's northeast corridor.[232]

Infiltration by Pakistan-based insurgents into India's border, particularly via the Line of Control in Kashmir, has been an unending problem for India. Such infiltration was cause for war in 1999 over the Kargil District of Ladakh, as well as for the abetment of the insurgency in Punjab through the 1980s. Narco-trafficking, arms smuggling, and the transfer of other materials are a day to day affair on the Indo-Pakistani frontier.

Logistical Issues

In addition to land migration and trafficking, *underground tunnels* may soon be dug into India from Pakistan and Bangladesh. These tunnels—already staples of borders such as those between the United States and Mexico,[233] Israel and Gaza, and Gaza and Egypt[234]—can be used to smuggle drugs, weapons, money (real and counterfeit) and people for both employment and conflict purposes.

They can also come to good use of the defence forces of the countries of the tunnels' origin. India itself has considered building deep tunnels across its borders with Pakistan and China. According to a proposal by the Indian Army Northern Command, "the use of tunnels would help in evading enemy satellites from gauging the exact troop strength and their position in the forward areas."[235]

On the issue of *maritime security,* India has long sought to solidify its hegemony over the Indian Ocean. The Indian Navy has been used in conventional and semi-conventional operations since Independence, namely the 1961 annexation of Goa in Operation Vijay, Operation Trident's offensive on Karachi during the 1971 War and the 1988 joint Operation Cactus with the Indian Air Force in the Maldives.

Since then, naval operations have been, and will continue to become, increasingly complex and decentralised, facing clandestine agents, non-state actors, or otherwise small-scale, potentially powerful agents. Pakistan-based terrorists such as the Lashkar-e-Tayyeba (LeT), and other networked organisations have developed sea-faring capacities to transport weapons and carry out attacks. Port security and the increasing importance of maritime straits in global trade in a more globalised Indian economy pose naval threats as well. The extension of Indian naval capacities beyond the Bay of Bengal, Arabian Sea, Gulf of Aden, and Strait of Malacca— "where 42 percent of pirate attacks took place in 2003"[236]—brings immense challenges from small, decentralised, non-state actors.

As technologies continue to evolve, and *space* is becoming a central realm of human activity, the 'superterraneous' is now being referred to as the "final frontier" of national security. Air space and its control has long been an element of national sovereignty, and will continue to be so. But the proliferation of satellites and space-based technology as tools of national communication, information procurement for commercial and intelligence purposes, war, energy acquisition, and other purposes is giving new dimensions to issues of control, infiltration, espionage and sovereignty.

The decentralisation of power away from governments and nation-states— what some might term the retreat of the state or a redefinition of sovereignty[237]—conflagrates these issues further. 'Market forces' drive this decentralisation, and make borders, physical, political and otherwise, blurry. Cross-border trade, as well as private (even joint-venture) ownership of various instruments of power—industry, technologies, etc—bring about a shift in the very definition of borders. As P.V. Indiresan has written,

> Indian policy-makers suffer from a fortress mentality: they believe that they will be safe behind high, impenetrable walls. In this era of high-speed communications, fortresses are obsolete; they offer no protection. Even if they do, they can do so only when the fortress wall is easily accessible from within but difficult to scale from outside. The fortresses that India builds are exactly of the opposite kind: India's boundaries are virtually inaccessible from within but are easily reached from outside. Just imagine a fortress wall that is 100 feet tall and unscalable looking from inside but only five feet high from outside and, therefore, easy to climb over! India's frontiers are like that—difficult to defend but easy for outsiders to nibble at with impunity. That is how India has lost much in the Kashmir Valley, in Ladakh and in Arunachal Pradesh. Unless India realizes the futility of keeping its frontiers inaccessible, it is liable to lose control of more territory all along its northeastern borders the same way it has lost elsewhere.[238]

Technological Drivers of Conflict

Cyber Warfare

With the increasing reliance on communication technologies for military, business, and even social operations throughout the globe, the *cyber warfare* threat looms large. This mode of attack can target both control systems and data.[239]

The former, control system attacks, includes attempts to disable or alter electronic systems that manage physical infrastructure such as power, water, and fuel supplies, communications, commercial and transportation systems of the military and civilian targets.

The latter, data-targeting, includes attempts to steal or corrupt information and information repositories, equipment disruption and 'Denial-of-Service' (DOS) attacks that can incapacitate both military and civilian (including private sector) infrastructure and even cripple certain economic sectors of the country.

Cyber war can also take the form of espionage via hacking against Indian government databases and information repositories, classified and unclassified, military and civilian.

Such hacking can alter the "balance of information and knowledge", tilting the perception and strategic landscape in an agent's favour.[240] Adversaries with whom the balance of forces is not favourable often prefer this type of perception manipulation. Clandestine and popular sub-national organisations, enabled by even commercially available hacking and encryption technologies, may favour these forms of perception manipulation through the means afforded by cyberspace.

As technologist Ravi Visvesvaraya Prasad writes, Pakistani hacker groups like

> Death to India, Kill India, and G-Force Pakistan openly circulate instructions for attacking Indian computers. The websites http://www.f**kindia.org, run by Nicholas Culshaw of Karachi, and http://www.f**kindia.com, run by Arshad Qureshi of Long Beach, California, contain malicious anti-Indian propaganda along with step-by-step instructions for hacking into thousands of Indian websites.[241]

Other forms of cyber warfare are often considered the tools primarily of nation-states, both overt adversaries and allies. James Mulvenon, Director of the Centre for Intelligence and Research, has said: "The Chinese are the first to use cyber attacks for political and military goals... Whether it is battlefield preparation or hacking networks connected to [heads of state], they are the first state actor to jump feet first into 21st century cyber warfare technology. This is clearly becoming a more serious and open problem."[242] While many countries conduct cyber espionage operations, many believe that the Chinese cyber war capacity is the most powerful. The Chinese have enabled cyber "sleeper-cells" that can target key industries and disrupt key systems if war ever demands it.[243]

Timothy Thomas of the US Army's Foreign Military Studies Office has said:

> China's leaders reckon that it can achieve hegemony in Asia only by integrating information warfare into its geopolitical strategies... "China is quickly integrating the latest information warfare techniques into its People's War concept. This development has been ignored by the West but will have far-reaching strategic and operational implications."[244]

The strategies that the People's Republic of China (PRC) has taken on in this regard are both centralised—having established branches of the military and civilian government agencies to deal specifically with cyber warfare—and decentralised through the recruitment of "gray hat" hackers – "cutting-edge techno patriots loosely affiliated with the Chinese government, but who are not formal agents of the state."[245]

Information and Its Security

With the growing centrality of information, as well as new technologies to enable access to it, issues related to *intelligence*, *privacy, identity-theft*, and *intellectual property rights* will become increasingly salient. Information plays a central role in the execution of nefarious activities. Firstly, more information has become more available in more places at faster rates. Secondly, the technologies for procuring and processing this information have improved and will continue to do so. Whether the information-processing tools of governments will be able to keep up with the capacities of micro level (individual and group) information dissemination remains to be seen.

Within democracies, a struggle exists between the capacities of governments and intelligence agencies, private citizens and nefarious agents who may be a part of citizenry or wholly separate. On one level, with more information driving social change as well as criminal activity, governments may not be able to keep pace. On another, new surveillance instruments and technologies such as data mining enable governments and even private sector firms to access this information with greater efficiency. The legal issues of *privacy* and *identity-theft* become increasingly salient in this light. While technologies have often been referred to as harbingers of information sharing and transparency,[246] the level of that transparency for private citizens and governments will bring with it philosophical, legal, and political debates, may cause tumult and, in extreme cases, backlash.

Moreover, as information becomes the backbone of more and more social, military and particularly economic activity, the *ownership* of information and its usage—i.e. intellectual property rights—can become sources of legal, political, and violent conflict. Conflict over information, increasingly a resource unto itself, may well come to define the tenor of conflict in certain realms.

The relative dearth of open source data on the implications of cyber warfare and information security in India, as well as a number of publicised security breaches in the public and private sectors,[247] suggest that the issue of information security has received insufficient attention. This is the case despite the Indian economy's heavy reliance on information technology and the emerging digitisation of information in both civilian and military realms. Such neglect does not bode well in the face of heightening reliance on emerging technological and web-based applications to business, military and government operations.

Emerging Technologies[248]

Longer-term, yet seismic shifts in the nature of technology include the convergence of four major areas: Nanotechnology, Biotechnology, Information Technology, and Cognitive/Neuro Technology (NBIC Convergence, or Converging Technologies).

Nanotechnology is the ability to manipulate the molecular properties of matter on the nano (10^{-9} metres) level, either to alter the structures of existing materials or develop wholly new materials beginning with the atom. Biotechnology refers to the capacity to modify biological organisms according to human needs, and more specifically to *genetic engineering*, in which organisms' genes are manipulated. Information technology encompasses the study, design, development, implementation, and management of computer-based systems that manage information, and the software applications and computer hardware that support these. Cognitive/neuro technology refers to hardware that affects the cognitive—psychological, philosophical, neurological, anthropological, social, and linguistic—capacities of humans.[249]

The convergence of these realms will initially bring about revolutionary breakthroughs in human capabilities. A brief overview of the implications of this convergence, according to the Proceedings of a December 2001 workshop on Convergent Technologies to Improve Human Performance organised by the United States National Science Foundation, includes the following categories:

- **Expanding Human Cognition and Communication:** Human cognitive and perceptual functions, communication between individuals and machines programmed with human-like characteristics, and understanding of human mental capacities through nanoscale analysis would be enhanced. Efforts to understand the structure and potential enhancement of the human mind, personal sensory device interfaces, and humanised technology would also be enabled.
- **Improving Human Health and Physical Capacities:** The control of cells, tissues and organs; conversion of bio-molecular signals and neural codes to man-made monitors to enable direct brain control of devices through neuromorphic engineering; nanoscale robots for unobtrusive medical intervention; brain-to-brain and brain-to-machine interfaces using connections to the human neural system; correcting handicaps and disabilities at the molecular level.[250]
- **Enhancing Group and Societal Outcomes:** Removing barriers to communication caused by physical disabilities, language differences, geographic differences, and variations in knowledge, thus, enhancing the effectiveness of social cooperation, creativity, and productivity in a networked society
- **National Security:** Converging technologies may enable data linkage and threat anticipation, uninhabited combat vehicles, war-fighter

> education and training, responses to chemical, biological, radiological and explosive threats, war-fighter systems, non-drug treatments to enhance human performance, exoskeletons for physical performance augmentation, and applications of brain-machine interfaces.[251]

A most controversial culmination of converging technologies is what has been referred to as *trans-humanism*—a movement that "seeks to liberate the human race from its biological constraints"[252] through the synergy of human biology with converging technologies. According to Nick Bostrom of Oxford University, trans-humans—and their later incarnations, 'post-humans'—can be either "completely synthetic artificial intelligences, or they could be enhanced, or they could be the result of making many smaller but cumulatively profound augmentations to a biological human."[253]

Many of these technologies may, 'enhance' human performance and capacity, as well as our ability to interact with non-social environments: resources can easily be made available through discovery of new sources (i.e. space) and the construction of new matter.

Such shifts can enable widespread self-sufficiency, the establishment of non-spatial social collectivities (beyond their current physical and web-based strata), and radical changes in the possible *sources* of people's conceptual understandings of themselves and of reality, compelling marked shifts in identities and new cultures.[254]

Far more profoundly, however, these technologies have the potential to alter the very realm of human existence. The very notions of human and humanity are challenged radically by converging technologies, as well as how those entities organise themselves and relate to one another.

In addition to the effects that such structural changes would have on human biology, society, and interaction with matter, the implications for global conflict are vast. As James Hughes of Trinity College has put it:

> The *coming technopolitical conflicts will be fought over the development, regulation, and accessibility of human enhancement technologies* and will bring to the table fundamentally different conceptions of citizenship, rights, and the polity. Technopolitics will be as profound [if not more profound]

> than the struggles between free marketers and Marxists, or secularists and fundamentalists, and will mix and blur among the 21st-century heirs of those battles. Unlike the struggle over trade union rights or gay marriage, however, the outcome of the technopolitical struggles will determine whether the human race itself [as it is today in its natural form] will have a future.[255]

Regardless of merits or demerits, converging technologies have institutional and intellectual support amongst even small minorities (most often government-funded endeavours in various pockets of only a handful of countries). Thus, the development, the rise of these technologies and their resultant social, physical, and security implications are all visible on the horizon. The equitable distribution and availability of these technologies will pose perhaps the greatest conceptual, social, and security threat therein. Polarisation between humans and "post-humans" in the coming century, and the conflict that emerges there from may well define the tenor of global society.

India, as a major producer and researcher of NBIC technologies, will certainly be at the crux of this global contingency. It must be cognisant of the challenges that come with these technologies.

The Environment, Climate Change and National Security

Climatic shifts have long had a profound effect on Indian security. The 2005 monsoon in Mumbai, for example, incapacitated the city, killed over 1,000 people, caused damage amounting to hundreds of crores, spawned health problems of epidemic proportions and rendered the city effectively quarantined. The annual visitations of floods, extreme heat, droughts and storms have caused death, destruction and disease and generally brought life to a stop in one region or the other of the country. Even a seemingly basic environmental issue such as access to clean, potable water has been a daily struggle for many, and has contributed to conflicts.

The conflict in Indian Punjab, for example, arguably traces its origins to the distribution of water resources between India and Pakistan, and Indian Punjab, Chandigarh, Kashmir, and Himachal Pradesh.[256] Moreover, water is at the core of the Kashmir conflict between India and Pakistan. Many of the rivers of the subcontinent's northern region flow from the mountains of the

Himalayas, pass through Kashmir, and flow into India and Pakistan (i.e. to both eastern and western Punjab), feeding the the agricultural and economic powerhouses of both the countries. In Pakistan, what is left of the Kashmiri river water flows into Sindh, causing tensions between western Punjab and Sindh. These contentions are, in turn, deflected onto the source of these rivers, namely Kashmir.[257]

However, environmental issues take on another dimension with *the global climate crisis.* A global scientific consensus[258] has demonstrated a causal relationship between anthropogenic (human-induced) emissions of greenhouse gases and a rise in global climate, which, in turn, has non-linear effects on environmental conditions throughout the world. Increasing carbon emissions by industrialisation throughout the world—from a few countries in particular—have created a radiative layer of carbon dioxide (CO2) around the earth

This layer adds to an already thick atmosphere, a combination that does not allow the sun's heat to escape into space, or the upper atmosphere, thereby raising global temperatures.

MICRO-MACRO INTERACTIONS

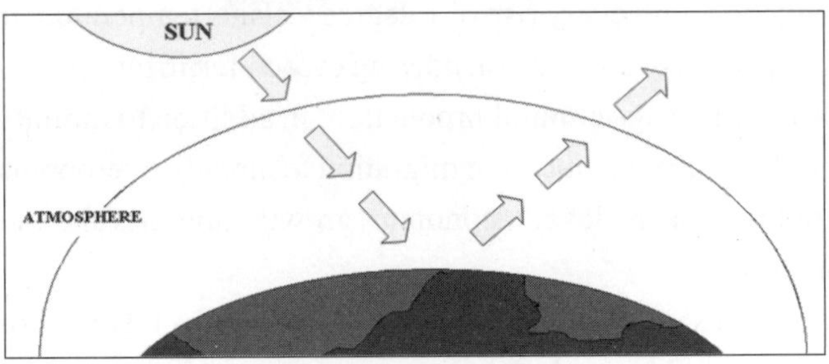

Pre-CO2 Atmosphere

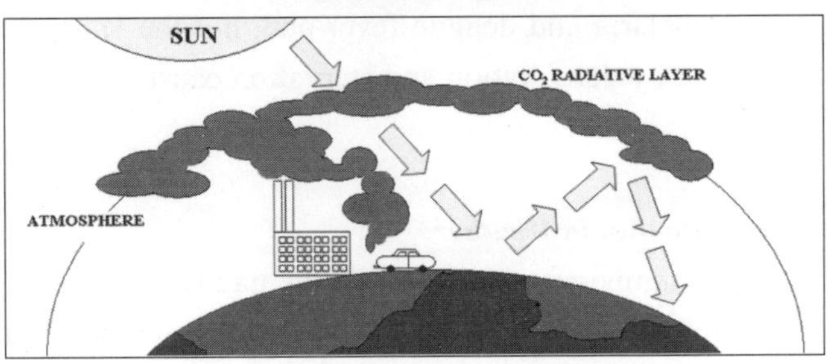

Post-Emission Atmosphere and Resultant Heat

In the Indian subcontinent in particular, the effects of climate change will manifest themselves in ways that will threaten scientific, geographic, and even *human* security. Moreover, the effects that climate change can have on *national security* are overwhelming. These dangers are particularly daunting to India, given its geographic location in the equatorial region of the world, adjacent to the Himalayan plateau, and India's role as home to a third of the world's poor.[259] Sources state that the world's poor are most vulnerable to the effects of climate change, having the least recourse from the status quo and minimal protection from environmental shifts.[260] The following discussion describes a number of likely scenarios for the effects of climate change on Indian human, national, and regional security.

Rising Temperature

A rise in temperature will lead to desertification, loss of arable land, and mass movements of regular migrants as well as refugees. For the farmers in the vast rural areas already hit by policy neglect and increased competition from global markets, climate change spells doom. The Indian Agriculture Research Institute (IARI) estimates the loss of "four to five million tons in wheat production with every rise of 1 degree Celsius temperature throughout the growing period, even after considering carbon fertilization."[261] A massive setback or failure in agricultural production, in addition to diminishing food supply, would precipitate massive migration to already overpopulated urban centres. India's macro-level economic growth and development would suffer immensely.

Within cities themselves, rising temperatures would overburden infrastructures such as electricity generation and spawn insect-borne diseases such as malaria and dengue fever and, not the least, the death of hundreds of people by dehydration and starvation caused by desertification and water loss.

Extremes and Anomalies in Weather

Changes in global temperature have offset the naturally occurring patterns of weather throughout the world. The southwestern summer monsoon and northeastern winter monsoon would be of greater intensity, threatening massive flooding. There will be an anomalous recurrence of typhoons, tsunamis, and other disasters, bringing with it death, disease destruction and displacement, and leading to exodus.

Rising Sea Levels

Due to the retreat of glaciers in Antarctica and the Arctic Circle, global sea levels are projected to rise by some 20 metres by the year 2100, depending on the rate of melting.[262] Submersion of islands and seashore areas of the land masses in the region would result in massive migration to higher lands. The President of Maldives, for example, has created an investment fund to buy land in neighbouring countries to resettle his country's citizens.[263]

The submersion of island territories (both Indian and foreign) as well as neighbouring states such as Bangladesh would prompt massive migration to and within India. In recent years, the coastline of Bangladesh has been receding, and has been exacerbated by flooding, tsunamis, and cyclones. Additionally, rising sea levels would cause the submersion of coastal areas, including urban centres like Mumbai.

Himalayan Glaciers

The Himalayan glaciers are melting at fast and faster rates. These glaciers source a vast majority of the rivers that flow not only into India, but throughout the rest of Asia. The Tibetan plateau (which includes glaciers that extend as far south as Nepal, Northern India and Northern Pakistan) has long been seen as a barometer of global climate conditions. Even if current warming trends remain constant (which is unlikely given their steady and anticipated rise), the plateau's glaciers could be reduced by a third by 2050 and by half by 2090, according to a 2007 survey conducted by the Remote Sensing Department of the China Aero Geophysical Survey.[264] This melting would result in a number of disastrous scenarios for India in particular. Owing to sudden and precipitous melting, extensive flooding in northern Indian rivers is anticipated. The aftermath will see a reversal. Slow depletion of these glaciers would greatly reduce the river water flow in north India, intensifying further the problem of river water scarcity.

Resource Wars

Resource availability is already a problem across the country, causing inter-state tensions over water-sharing rights. It was a central issue behind the troubles in Punjab and there has been trouble for the same reasons in the agricultural sectors of other states. In both the long and short terms, melting glaciers will result in situations close to water scarcity, badly affecting agriculture and livelihood, crippling power plants and erupting in tussles for water resources.

At the local level, water has been a distressing point of contention between villages and within cities. Water availability is scant and its distribution has long been inequitable and biased, however informally, by caste, linguistic, and other identity-based divisions.[265] Otherwise highly trusting communities have been heavily securitised due to issues over water availability and theft.

The effect of water availability not only for consumption, but also agriculture, electricity production, and the resultant migration will perforce escalate rural, urban and regional conflicts.

Domestically, water has long been a contentious issue and an igniter of conflict at both the local and regional levels. As Tibetan glaciers melt, rains fluctuate, river flows ebb, and fresh water becomes more and more scarce, water conflicts may become the rule of the day in the near future.

Conflicts and wars over resources such as water are often cloaked in the guise of identity or ideology-based conflicts. The occurrence of resource-based conflicts is rarely overt and is often difficult to discern. Thus, resource issues serve as multipliers, if not igniters, of political conflict.[266]

Internationally, the stakes are higher. Water is at the core of the Kashmir conflict between India and Pakistan. The three western rivers of Kashmir— Indus, Jhelum, and Chenab—and the three eastern rivers—Sutlej, Beas, and Ravi—are all sourced in China and thereafter flow through Jammu and Kashmir. The Indus Water Treaty of 1960[267] gave near exclusive control over the three western rivers to Pakistan and over the eastern ones to India. The political status of the water may have remained generally unchanged since then, but it has constantly been at the centre of both the countries' strategic thinking. The effects of Tibetan glacier retreat and the resultant fall in the rivers' flows would hit Pakistan's economy in particular and could bring already tenuous relations with India to the threshold of conflict.

The sharing and joint management of water resources with Nepal is again a complex issue. Key problem areas are: (1) water sources themselves are becoming scarce due in part to rising populations; (2) glitches in joint-management have led to flooding in both countries; (3) political contentions over water management and resource control; and (4) damming of Nepali rivers for purposes of hydroelectric power generation. Once the climate change-induced deluge of rivers and the subsequent river water depletion occur, this already thorny bilateral issue will get bogged down in further complications. The dialogue even holds the possibility of becoming a trialogue, given the potential Chinese role in Nepal's economic and infrastructure development.

Flooding in the Ganga River Delta coupled with rising sea levels has proved to be a disaster for Bangladesh, leading to uncontrollable and illegal mass migration to India; some 6,000 people illegally enter India every day.[268] This has prompted India to begin building a long stretch of fencing to keep Bangladeshis out.

Given the long-term prospects of resource depletion in the Tibetan plateau itself, China has considered diverting Tibetan waters to its own eastern provinces. The river has been a cause of tension between China and India, including over the lack of information-sharing about climatic situations in Tibet, which later caused flooding in India and Bangladesh. Should the Chinese divert the Tibetan waters without consulting New Delhi, it could result in a massive—and *unexpected*—ebb in water to India's north, hampering hydroelectric power generation,[269] causing water famine conditions both within India and other countries in South Asia, and damaging India's relations with neighbouring countries. Moreover, the already tense relations between India and China could deteriorate to war-like situations, making political contentions over Arunachal Pradesh, for example, pale in comparison.

Key regions in which water availability may be highly correlated with conflict are: Kashmir and Punjab around the tributaries of the Indus River; northern central India around the Ganges and Yamuna Rivers; northeastern India around the Dhang River; central India at the Godavari and; south India at the Cauvery River.[270]

Rivers in India and Key Conflict Zones[271]

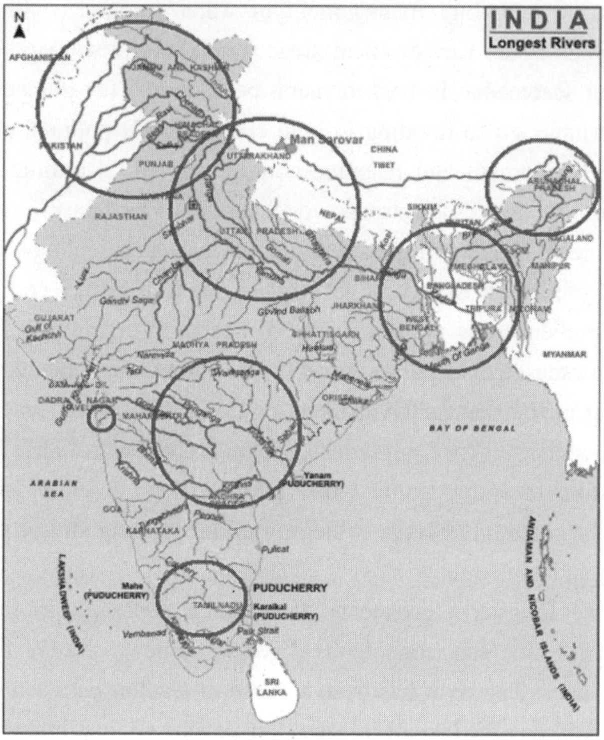

Governance of the Environment[272]

A key debate in the management of climate change has been the choice between *mitigation* and *adaptation.* Proponents of mitigation hold the view that since climate change is a cause-and-effect phenomenon, the *causes* of climate change—namely, the emission of greenhouse gases—can and should be reduced in order to minimise the consequences. The argument for adaptation, on the other hand, is that it is too late to minimise the causes of climate change and humans must, therefore, adapt to the effects.

On the whole, global and regional frameworks have attempted to work towards mitigation, while the few local and national plans that exist focus on adaptation. In all practicality, both are necessary, particularly for India, where the technological resources for sufficient adaptation are minimal but doing so is particularly vital, and mitigation efforts are necessary to prevent the most disastrous long-term effects of climate change.

The 1990s saw a round of environmental negotiations that ended with the failed Kyoto Protocol of the United Nations Framework Convention on Climate Change (UNFCCC). The primary contention over the treaty, which led to its failure was the "Common but Differentiated Responsibility" clause of the protocol, which stated that the largest share of historical greenhouse gas emissions have been from the developed countries in the course of their development; per capita emissions in the developing countries remain relatively low; and global emissions from the developing countries will grow as the countries meet their development and economic needs. The major developing countries, such as China and India—the first and third-largest net-emitters of greenhouse gases—were accordingly not included in any numerical limitations, which American legislators rejected, deeming the clause unfair to the US economy.[273]

Accordingly, as per the status quo, global greenhouse gas emissions continue to rise at increasing rates, accompanied by a concomitant rise in global temperatures. China, India, and other developing countries have firmly held the view that mandating emission caps would be harmful for their economic development, claiming such a move was the legacy of the unjust colonial system of industrialisation and development that favoured the developed countries and excused their past carbon emissions.

This is in many ways a legitimate position, because (a) in the redistribution of ecological space, development imbalances must be contrasted with greater energy *efficiency* and new technologies; (b) the doctrine of "common but differentiated responsibility" is sound, as is; (c) the Linking Clause of the UNFCCC, which states that compliance by developing countries is contingent on compliance by developed countries.[274] Indeed, environmentalists such as Sunita Narain have argued that global environmental frameworks must be based on paradigms of global justice if they are to have any effective legitimacy.[275]

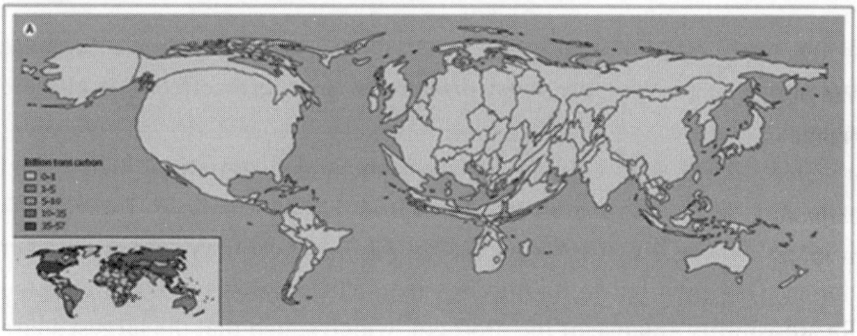

This image from *The Lancet*[276] represents which countries are more responsible for climate change as a result of greenhouse emissions over the period of 1950 to 2000.

However, some, such as Lavanya Rajamani of the Centre for Policy Research, argue that while "India's position is legitimate, *it is not sagacious*." Poorer states in the tropical belt—such as India—and in particular the poorest within them, including the 35 percent of the country that lives on less than one dollar a day, will feel the effects of climate change disproportionately. Climate change will wreak havoc of the sort articulated above on countries like India, with 1/6th of the world's population, while having relatively milder short-term effects on developed countries or those in the northern hemisphere. The latter, accordingly, have lesser short-term incentives for preventive action, while the former will suffer the immediate consequences.[277]

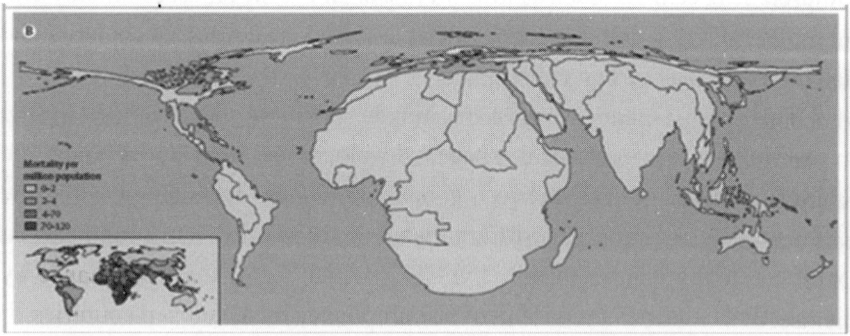

This image from The Lancet[278] represents which countries will be harmed most by climate change, namely "the regional distribution of four climate-sensitive health consequences (malaria, malnutrition, diarrhea, and inland flood-related fatalities)."

Facing more immediate, dire consequences, India faces greater pressure than other countries to manage (i.e. adapt to) the local challenges of climate change. *Political and logistical agreements that* ***preemptively*** *address issues of water sharing and joint resource management (coupled, of course, with technological adaptation) should be at the forefront of India's adaptation policy at the regional, provincial, and local levels.*

On the regional level, a number of key issues exist insofar as management and adaptation are concerned. Refugees fleeing neighbouring countries afflicted by changing weather patterns—primarily Bangladesh—will be a key international consequence of climate change. While economic and security concerns have already compelled such migration, climatic shifts will turn migration into a large-scale exodus. While international conventions securing the rights of political refugees exist, no such standards or laws discussing necessary provisions for climate or *environmental* refugees have been established.[279]

Fencing off the border with Bangladesh to check migration has been touted as a method of addressing the issue.[280] There are, of course, concerns regarding governance of the fence (namely, bribery that allows migrants transport), the sufficiency of its length and height, military stand-offs between border patrols, and political-diplomatic considerations. But these considerations aside, the very efficacy of the fence in managing 'climate refugees' is questionable, given the alternatives that the traffickers and illegal migrants have, for example, underground tunnels. Moreover, it is doubtful that the fence would withstand the massive refugee influx that is anticipated to occur in the wake of the most disastrous climate change scenarios.

In India's northwest, the Indus Waters Treaty that has kept the tenuous, relative peace over resources between India and Pakistan over the last half century threatens to collapse in light of climatic shifts. The control of Delhi and Islamabad over the six rivers has also meant that the Kashmiris themselves have been denied sufficient access to water since 1960.[281] Indian plans to dam Kashmiri rivers—for the recent Kishanganga hydroelectric power plant, for example[282]—have often upset Pakistan, which fears a reduction of water for its own use. These concerns would be compounded further by the retreat of rivers. In any future political, diplomatic, or other moves on the Kashmir issue, water and climate management should be central themes.

Seminal to the regional governance of the environment is India's relationship with China. Their positions on global climate mitigation frameworks are in essence similar. This, in conjunction with the implications of the Tibetan Plateau on the whole of Asia, trends towards the recession of its glaciers, and China's efforts to divert Tibetan water sources to eastern China (to the detriment of South Asia), mandates the need for the two Asian giants to formulate a common framework. A strong power dynamic, however, exists between the two countries: given Chinese control over Tibet and the water sources therein, South Asia may appear to be beholden to Chinese actions. Recognising this dynamic, climate change is an issue on which the two otherwise competing countries may be able to develop a broader cooperative framework that includes cooperation in, and transfer of, technology, as well as political agreements on water sharing.

On the domestic front, so as to avert internal contests over water rights, national, state, and local authorities must also play a part in the climate management process. Investing in alternative energies and technologies and setting national and local targets for carbon emission reduction are certainly seminal. However, some more innovative and radical approaches are necessary.

As a result of development and growth patterns, urbanisation is a key demographic trend in India. Thereafter, rapid urbanisation contributes to increases in motorisation (more vehicles per capita),[283] which, in turn, leads to greater fossil fuel consumption. According to a report by the International Energy Agency,

> The share of global CO2 emissions in cities is higher than that for energy use [in rural areas] because as developing countries urbanize, they tend to shift from biomass and waste (assumed to be relatively CO2 neutral) to more CO2-intensive energy resources. Since city residents also tend to consume more energy than rural residents, they, therefore, emit more CO2 per capita.[284]

Efforts must be made to mitigate urbanisation itself, which comes as a result of inequitable development patterns.[285] Moreover, urban infrastructures that emphasise fossil fuel consumption—namely, a neglect for effective public transport and roads that encourage and often necessitate a reliance on cars for efficient, comfortable transportation—must be altered in favour of more efficient, effective mass mobility rather than motorisation.

Lastly, adaptation on the local, domestic level is necessary. Although adaptive technologies will develop and mitigation efforts will be encouraged, domestic and local deficiencies in water and resource availability are *inevitable*. Resource sharing agreements that preemptively address water management and sharing at the inter-state, inter-district, inter-community, and intra-community levels, and communication mechanisms that enable the implementation of these agreements are vital.

Poverty and Economics in the Realm of Security

Economics as Instruments of State Policy

With the liberalisation and integration of global markets, economics has come to play an increasingly central role in the realm of security. India's anticipated global 'rise' itself is the outcome of the fact that, next to China, it has the highest economic growth rate in the world.

On a macro-scale, a decline in its economic clout may lead to the waning of a state's political or diplomatic influence in the world. As India's global position has now firmed, comparisons with countries such as China are inevitable. Economic clout has enabled India to invest in various sectors, as well as extend its diplomatic influence to countries across the world over the last decades. If India's growth and resultant global economic clout fail to keep it afloat or ahead of its potential rivals—and it lacks a coherent economic strategy that is politically viable and favorable to constituent parties—global rivals may usurp India's political and diplomatic position.

Sovereign Wealth Funds (SWFs), i.e., state-owned investment funds made up of financial assets of other countries' currency, can be a strong economic tool vis-à-vis other countries. While India currently does not own any SWFs—most foreign reserves are held in low-yield, low-risk government securities[286]—the political leverage that these funds provide for the Gulf countries and China, particularly vis-à-vis the US, are a sign of the sort of economic tools to come.[287]

Investments by both the private and public sectors provide the initial boost and leverage to a country's economic development and also pave the way for additional engagement. Likewise, economic development assistance can serve as a powerful tool of power projection as well as influence in a recipient country and soft power around the world. Depending on the type of assistance, the investment can be either symbiotic or parasitic. India's ventures in Africa, for example, have been quite exemplary in this regard. Its development projects in that continent bring employment for indigenous workforces and infrastructure projects have been more even-handed in the benefits they provide to local populations. While such investments benefit the Indian economy itself, symbiotic relations, coupled with Indian Diasporas in those countries, have given India a soft-power amongst many people in Africa, and open up the prospect of closer political and strategic relations.[288]

This symbiosis can be contrasted with investments in Africa by China and the Western countries, which often import their own labour and invest in sectors that favour status quo governments that often subjugate their citizens, engendering popular ill will for the donor country.[289]

This process creates investment-development schemes that often yoke recipient countries to donors in such ways that recipients become dependent on donors and are forced to acquiesce to their political pressures.[290] While such relations have enabled investing powers to extract resources, capital, and political influence for their own gain in the short to medium-term, in the medium to long-term, the latter have suffered political and physical[291] fallouts from the negative perceptions that result from such parasitic development aid.

Conflict Economies

Mismanaged aid and development money given to targeted regions can often have the unintended consequences of financing leaders and propagating insurgencies. Moreover, due in large part to the inextricability of illegal activities from those that are legal, whole sectors of conflict based economies can emerge and sustain themselves. Conflict itself becomes so entrenched in the market and in civil society—and vice versa—that freeing the society as a whole from its grip becomes a near impossible task. It makes life impossible and imperils the of livelihood of ordinary, citizens (non-combatants), caught in a situation where the economy, civil society, and the conflict reinforce one another.

As Ajai Sahni of the Institute for Conflict Management writes of the insurgencies in northeast India,

> A complex collusive arrangement between various legitimate power elites and terrorist groupings exists in every single terrorism-affected State [in northeast India], and this arrangement facilitates a continuous transfer of resources into the 'underground economy of terrorism'. In contrast to the common perception of terrorist activity as violent confrontation with the government, there is a more insidious subversion of the established order through a consensual regime against a backdrop of widespread breakdown of law and order, and terrorist groupings have demonstrated their preference towards 'systemic corruption', rather than the dismantling or destruction of the prevailing political order.[292]

In addition to maintaining and propagating existing sources of conflict, conflict economies divert a great deal of resources from the intended investment targets— sustainable, development-oriented sectors—the *opportunity cost* of such conflict economies is immense.[293]

The Military-Industrial Complex

Corruption that has affected lower levels of government in India has not left the defence forces untouched. In the 1990s, the media, the government and civil society exposed a number of high profile names in a kickbacks case involving defence procurement. Politicians, it was revealed, had procured cheap, poor quality, obsolete MiG planes from Russia in return for "personal financial remuneration".[294]

Such a coupling of decision-making and defence procurement can, however, reach greater proportions. In his 1992 piece on Indian strategic thought, George Tanham states that one of India's goals in its rise to great power status was to have its own "Military-Industrial Complex" (MIC). MIC refers to the entangling of the military, industry and government in economic ventures that produces a self-reinforcing cycle: the government supports military development, which, in turn, supports the defence industry, which then financially backs the government (often by lobbying politicians), thus, creating a feedback cycle.

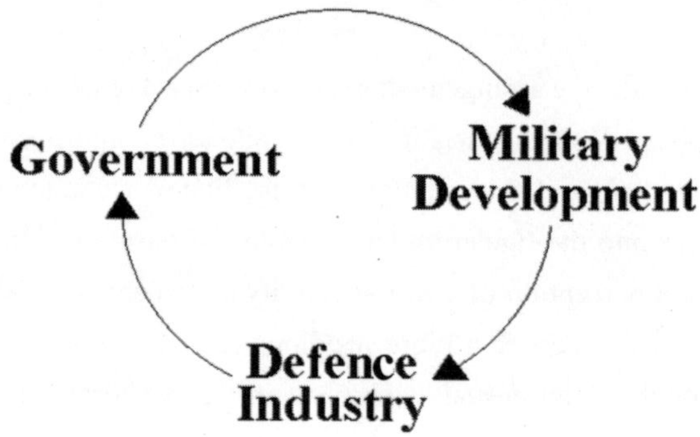

Such an economic sub-system does not yet exist in India because its indigenous defence industry does not exist on such a large scale. But it has a strong presence in states like the US and Israel. In those countries, the MIC has given rise to robust defence industries that provide munitions and even civilian technology to both domestic and foreign customers, thus, filling up the country's coffers.

However, such a complex has also meant that military industries exert an unwarranted level of influence on government policy: defence contractors closely linked to the government can encourage excessively militaristic policies with an eye only to their own profits.[295] Investments are often made in unnecessary equipment, and strategic decisions are beholden to the economic motives of the defence industry.

The economic and political effects of the MIC in the US have been substantial. Budgetary decisions have yielded to military concerns and funds have been diverted at the cost of civilian needs.[296] Even unnecessary, politically motivated appropriations of government spending are made for projects that are chiefly intended to benefit particular constituents, campaign contributors, or other vested interests.[297]

Moreover, the military-industrial complex, given its institutional preference for defence investment, poses a major challenge to a holistic understanding of national security, which needs to go *beyond* the narrow field of national defence—a necessary conceptual expansion in the emerging strategic environment that would put more emphasis on civilian governance in security affairs.[298]

India has, thus, far been relatively immune to such an unwelcome influence on its governmental decision-making. But, as US President Dwight D. Eisenhower warned in the 1950s against its emergence in the US, the Indian government must be cognisant of the challenges MICs can pose to its own thinking and action. Such a threat refers not only to the potential emergence of India's own military-industrial complex, but to the implications of *other countries'* MICs on India's own weapons procurement and geopolitical strategies. The MICs of other countries can influence them to sell even obsolete or unnecessary equipment to customer nations, benefiting suppliers' economies while holding recipients' decision-making hostage to their purchases, favouring the employment of weaponry and more military-prone decisions.[299]

Urbanisation, Migration and Development

A rise in urbanisation can be anticipated from the current demographic and economic trends in India.[300] This can come about through two primary scenarios: (1) migration to, and expansion of, existing urban centres; and (2) development of new and alternate urban centres.[301] Path dependencies favouring existing urban areas and insufficient investment in 'alternate' urban areas suggest that the former scénario will take precedence and that current urban centres will become even more densely populated.

Failures or weaknesses in the agricultural sector, stemming from increased global competition, domestic policy neglect, diminished water and other drivers may compel large-scale migration from rural to urban areas. Already stressed urban infrastructures will undergo further strains due to increased population pressures. If urban development and management prove incapable of dealing with these pressures, infrastructural deficiencies would cause disasters and physical harm to citizens.

Urban and rural areas undergo self-reinforcing feedback cycles linking development, migration, and the availability of employment opportunities. In rural areas, economic opportunities are scant, a problem that has been exacerbated by global economic trends such as industrial exploitation of ecosystems. This lack of development and infrastructure deters further investment in rural areas, a deficit that compels people to migrate to urban areas in search of employment. As there are fewer people in rural areas, there is even less of an incentive to invest in them, compelling still more people to migrate to cities.

This keeps rural areas stagnant and underdeveloped, while the residents emigrate. This rural plight, particularly when contrasted with booming opportunities available in cities, can lead to overt conflict against a seemingly negligent or otherwise ineffective state and mainstream society, as is evident in the Naxal-affected regions of India.

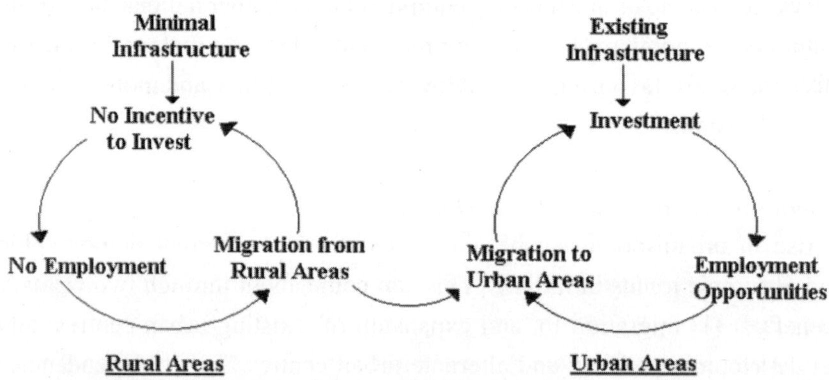

In urban areas, economic opportunities and investment exist, which compels people to migrate to urban centres. This job motivated migration to, and greater population in, urban areas drives further investment in urban centres.

At a point, "chaotic urbanisation"—overpopulation of cities, overstrain and failure of infrastructure, excessive poverty and diminished employment and development opportunities— may emerge in a way that any efforts of planners, governments, developers, the private sector, and residents themselves to manage problems may be in vain. When chaotic urbanisation is compounded with identity-based grievances, the result can be a volatile, violent mix.

Poverty and Economic Stratification

Both the government and the moderately well off middle class society—the so-called mainstream – would appear to be in a denial of the increasing stratification of Indian society based on economic disparities. This stratification can precipitate scenarios of potent enmity and sub-national conflict.

Recent historical examples of regional poverty and economic mismanagement leading to mass upheavals are Kashmir, the northeast, and most prominently, the Naxalite movement in the eastern and central regions of India.[302] The potential for other regions to be engulfed in similar violence—particularly those coupled with identity-based conflicts —is large. Likewise, as urban poverty increases, there may be a burgeoning of street crime, extremist political movements and organised crime operating from urban hubs.[303]

The rise and strength of the Naxalite movement reiterates a fact of human existence: poverty enslaves; extreme poverty rebels. As *The Economist* has reported:

> In the tiny, dirt-poor villages scattered through the forest[s] of Andhra Pradesh, Orissa and Chhattisgarh], *the Indian state is almost invisible*. There are no roads, waterpipes, electricity or telephone lines. In another village a teacher does come, but, in the absence of a school, holds classes outdoors. Policemen, health workers and officials are never seen. *The vacuum is filled by Naxalite committees*, running village affairs and providing logistic support to the fighters camping in the forest.[304]

Many have described how Maoist enterprises have essentially taken over the administrative role in a large number of districts of eastern India. Naxal forms of tax collection and wealth distribution, efficient judicial processes and prosecution such as the *jan adalats*,[305] policing, employment and economic growth and other forms of governance have emerged "in the administrative and political vacuum that extends over vast areas of India, where the state has systematically and chronically failed to provide the goods and services it is required to."[306]

Beyond direct conflict driven by poverty itself, the space of opportunity for impoverished and hopeless persons to be exploited by nefarious sub-national groups and state-actors such as Pakistan's Inter-Services Intelligence agency, remains immense. This nexus is not unrelated to the networked organisation discussed at the micro level.

In the case of the Naxalite movement of eastern India, the Naxals conduct "detailed socio-economic surveys…before starting operations in a target area, helping to identify grievances they can exploit."[307]

Urban poverty has also been fully manipulated. Slums have been linked to both religious extremism—particularly Hindu fundamentalism—and strong patron-client couplings that form organised crime networks.

The impoverished masses in India are left bereft of the most basic social services. Their very existence as Indian citizens is not registered, or even known by the Indian government. These persons are also out of the scope of accountability to governance that those services provide, in that no documentation of their existence exists.[308] Quite naturally, they are easy game for recruiters of criminal organisations, either for direct participation in nefarious activities or for obstruction of justice (i.e., confessing for a crime committed by someone else in exchange for financial remuneration) without being held accountable by the judicial system.

Further economic stratification that threatens manipulation or violent conflict would surface along three major divides:

- *regional* level (economic disparities among various regions of India);
- *urban-rural* (economic schism divides between urban and rural populations); and
- *urban poverty* (economic divides within single localities).

In a country in which an estimated 456 million people—42 per cent of the population and one-third of the *world's* poor[309]—live below the poverty line, it is highly likely that these divisions will flare up into conflicts. The Naxalite corridor that has spread to a third of India, from Bihar to Andhra Pradesh; endemic poverty and economic and developmental disparities throughout the country, coupled with divided state-federal bureaucracies and governance structures[310]; and competing domestic nationalisms add further fuel to the fire.[311]

The Nation and the State in the 21st Century: Perceptions at the Micro-Macro Level

The idea of the 'Indian' nation is very new. While some allude to the millennia-old notion of *Akhanda Bharat* as evidence of a millennia-old nation, the very idea of the 'nation' as a source of identity, and nationalism as a means of defending it, only arose in Europe with the 1648 Westphalia Treaty and was solidified in the succeeding centuries. Other versions of 'nations' and nationalism arose only subsequently—largely in the colonial and post-colonial periods—in other parts of the world, including India.

In India, the *nation* needed creation, definition, accommodation, and wide scale acceptance in a post-Independence period of many challenges. Ethno-linguistic nationalisms abounded, while many in the new nation felt that much of the subcontinent (East and West Pakistan) rejected the very feasibility of the idea of a secular, united India. Such major blows to the confidence of any proposed nation, particularly at its inception, can be traumatic.

The 'Idea of India' has been strengthened and reformulated in many ways since, but has suffered many setbacks as well. In the last 20 years in particular, the pulls of globalisation have exacerbated the initial divisions (including partition). Pan-Islamism, Hindu 'revivalism,' ethnic Diasporas, economic and political autonomy movements, insurgencies, and various non-state and non-national identities have all been reignited by globalisation.

Since the end of the bipolar Cold War era, as political scientist Dr. James Rosenau has written :

> ...global structures have undergone a transformation in which the state-centric system has been weakened by the advent of a new, multi-centric system that has expanded enormously as the number and variety of spheres

> of authority have proliferated….I have called it a "bifurcated system" in which the state-centric and multi-centric worlds sometimes cooperate, often conflict, and endlessly interact. The emergence of the multi-centric world derives in good part from the new microelectronic technologies that have rendered individuals and communities more interdependent. Global television, the Internet, the fax machine, the cell phone, and a host of other technologies that have flowered since 1991 have, as *The Economist* once put it, led to "the death of time and distance."[312]

These technologies, the collapse of the bipolar global order (and of the authority structures associated with it), the retreat of the state from the lives of citizens and other factors associated with 'globalisation' have contributed to the "disaggregation of authority," [313] around the world, in which conventional sources of authority and allegiance—the state, status quo political ideologies, traditional leaders, and others—have begun to diminish in influence.

In the light of this 'crisis of authority'—in which these traditional sources of authority have become unable to frame and act upon goals and populations have become disillusioned with conventional centres of influence—new sources of authority arise. This process has been bolstered in large part by the rise in availability of information about new sources of authority, through integrative technologies.

In his *Imagined Communities*, nationalism scholar Benedict Anderson posits a correlation between print-media and national identity formulation in Europe. Fifteenth century Europe's ability to understand the complexity of the world increased exponentially through the emergence of print-capital and the newspaper, technologies that described multiple, simultaneously occurring, geographically separate events. The newspaper made individuals aware of events and people that existed at the same time as themselves. This awareness—a change from the conventional linear world-view propagated by Christendom—compelled people to identify with or against the simultaneous events and people about whom they had information. As a result of this common identification, *nationalism* was born.[314]

The effects of print-capital on nationalism—through knowledge of simultaneously occurring events and existing people—are perhaps repeating themselves with 21st century information and communications technologies that relay almost real-time occurrences across large distances. The knowledge of people and happenings throughout the world at a nearly instantaneous rate is in many ways a resurgence of the 15th century European phenomenon. People are able to learn about, and communicate and identify with those even on the other side of the world; the number of long-distance ties has increased and their strength has been enhanced.

In India, much of the void of electoral politics and state structures has been filled by sub-groupism and the reinvocation of historical allegiances, information about which has been spread by new technologies.

The rise of pan-Islamic thinking, in which a global *Ummah*, or community of believers takes precedence over allegiance to state or national alliances, has been bolstered immensely. Earlier, many Muslims within state boundaries connected to an *Ummah* only spiritually and through the *Hajj* pilgrimage in Mecca, as well as through smaller-scale Muslim networks such as Sufi orders and schools of jurisprudence.[315] However, pan-Islamic thinking, which often circumvents conventional sources of authority such as the state, has come to prominence, particularly in the last decades, largely in response to, and abetted by, the processes of globalisation and communications technologies.[316] Muslims from Philadelphia to Rabat, Leeds to Lahore, Amman to Mindanao, have been able to communicate and identify with one another. The ignited allegiances that followed were outside the realm of the nation-state.[317]

A process parallel to the Islamic phenomenon detailed above emerged in India with the rise of "Hindutva" politics in the wake of globalisation. The weakening of the conventional authority of the Congress Party in the mid-1980s contributed to a vacuum in power and public allegiances. Hindu organisations, both religious and radical, facilitated by these systemic shifts and a media strategy enabled by the technologies of globalisation[318],were able to step into the fray.[319] By the late 1980s and early 1990s, Hindutva political parties were making major electoral gains, and in 1996, the Bharatiya Janata Party (BJP), a party tied to Hindutva principles and organisations, formed a coalition government and later ruled from 1998 to 2004 for the first time since Independence. Again, allegiances and authority structures outside of conventional power sources had emerged.[320]

On sub-national levels, nativist (*Bhumiputra*) movements, ethno-linguistic, and other identity-based campaigns have been reignited both by systemic shifts and crises of authority. These have manifested in, for example, a strengthening and expansion of the Naxalite movement in eastern India; the increase in popular power of nativist parties such as the Shiv Sena and Maharashtra Navnirman Sena (MNS) in Mumbai and Maharashtra; and a resurgence of northeast insurgencies.

A strengthening of the organisational capacities of Diasporas has also contributed to the disaggregation of conventional authority in the Indian nation-state. As Yossi Shain, a scholar of Diaspora politics, has articulated, the role of the nation-state is in defining the nexus between nation and citizenship; Diasporas, however, exist within the nation, but outside the state.[321] Diaspora members, equally affected by authority crises on a more global, multi-dimensional scale, have experienced their own identity-based resurgences and been able to organise themselves politically and financially, and enhance communications and coordination with communities in their countries of origin, all due to the tools of globalisation.[322] These tools have enabled Diaspora members to organise themselves politically and financially in their host countries, while influencing politics and society in their countries of origin, often through etho-nationalist and other identity-based movements in the homeland itself.

These and other factors may compound to create the ultimate stress that many countries face today: *reconciling the political-geographic* ***state*** *with an identity-based* ***nation***. India in particular—as a relatively young post-colonial nation-state with a multi-ethnic population of over one billion people of fragmented economic status, a democratic form of governance, in transition to a free-market economic system, and tremendously weak processes of governance and policy implementation that would otherwise serve to reinforce the cohesion of the *nation* through public services—faces a challenge perhaps greater than any of its closest analogues.

There has been no multi-ethnic state in the world that has fully and successfully managed its nation thus far.[323] Meanwhile, various other '*fragmegrative*' challenges—those in which fragmentation and integration occur simultaneously— described in this text affect different scales of society in diverse ways. All of these can exacerbate further the tensions between nation and state.

Central to the task of ensuring the security and integrity of India and its population will be to effectively manage the *idea* of India in an era of competitive nationalisms, and keeping it as *credibly inclusive* as possible. An effective resolution between nation and state remains perhaps the greatest challenge to the integrity of the Indian Union, the safety and prosperity of its people, and perhaps even the security of the world.

Conclusion: Managing Security in a Complex Age*

In the age of globalisation, complex new forms of social organisation have emerged, in which interconnectivity and change have become the norm. On the micro level (individuals and groups), networked organisation and deficiencies in governance themselves pose security threats. On the macro level (nation-states and international systems), there are a number of challenges, but it is up to India itself to define and realise its own role in the international system and to *create* opportunities therein. On the scale of interactions between these levels, a number of compounding, interacting threats exist, all of which will require multi-pronged, concerted solutions.

A Complex Era

Emerging security threats are highly complex: networked and interactive, as well as dynamic and evolving. Globalisation and its tools have empowered both sub-national actors and states, thus, creating two worlds—that of individuals and groups, and that of states and the international system—that constantly influence one another. Through these and other interactions, the challenges that all of these pose are themselves *networked*. A change in some elements or their relationships produce changes in other parts of the system; chains of consequences extend "over time and many areas" and the effects of even a single action are always great in number, so much so that "we can never merely do one thing."[324]

---

* The author is indebted to Leon Fuerth and the author's work with his 'Project on Forward Engagement' for the intellectual foundations of this chapter. Please see www.forwardengagement.org for more information.

Moreover, individuals, groups, states, and international systems are highly *adaptive* and *evolve* in the light of the changing circumstances of the systems in which they exist.

Two conceptual changes that this new era enhances are *aggregation* and *positive feedback*. Agents and events can pick up and react to signals from one another, exponentially amplifying the threat that is posed by any one. Lone threats can have interactive consequences and feed off one another, serving as *threat multipliers*.

The Punjab insurgency of the 1980s is a prime example of the way various drivers can emerge, interact, and aggregate. The insurgency is commonly seen through three lenses: identity, law enforcement, and external influence.

- **Identity and Fundamentalism**: Khalistan, as a Sikh homeland, it is commonly held, had its origins in pre-Partition India, the creation of the Indian Punjab state, and was exacerbated further by weak Centre-state relations. All of these gave rise to radical religious fundamentalism that moved people to violence.
- **Law Enforcement**: Second, the lens propounded by the accounts K.P.S. Gill[325] and Julius Ribeiro,[326] the two Directors General (DGs) of Police who were credited with bringing the insurgency to an end, was that of law enforcement. Before their deputation, it is said, law enforcement did not respond to terrorism and insurgent violence with a sufficiently hard hand.
- **External Interference**: Enmity with Pakistan compelled the latter to support and train Khalistani militants, thus, strengthening their activities against India.

However, a few other factors contributed to the emergence of, support for, and prolongation of the insurgency

- **Environmental Factors**: The trifurcation of Punjab state in 1966 lessened Punjabi state control over the flows of, the rivers Sutlej, Beas, and Ravi into the region while increasing central government control over river management.[327] This diminution of control over water access, coupled with a slow recession of the rivers themselves, depletion of ground water aquifers, and a weakening monsoon contributed to the downfall of what many have called the unsustainability of the Green Revolution, ultimately causing frustration amongst Punjabi farmers.[328]

- **Economic Factors**: Due to environmental issues brought about by Punjab's trifurcation as well as the Green Revolution, subsidies were being withdrawn by the Centre and prices were decreasing. Moreover, migration to Punjab by people from states that were less economically prosperous began to strain capacities, opportunities and development in Punjab itself, bringing about resentment amongst the natives. Many also argue that the Green Revolution wound up empowering owners of large tracts of land at the expense of smaller farmers.[329]

These individual factors served as drivers that interacted and amplified the others' effects, the aggregate product of which was a large-scale insurgency. While the common narrative, described above, stated that attrition-based confrontation ended the insurgency, economic and political changes may have mitigated the environmental stresses on the population, while development in other states minimised migration to Punjab, easing economic strains and political tensions resulting from them.

In an era of globalisation, the very notion of security prioritisation becomes difficult, as the "either this issue or that" thinking of the past has given way to "both this issue and that" problems that can enhance the effects of one another when in simultaneous occurrence.[330]

This aggregation has accelerated further due to economic integration, globalisation and communications technologies, and taken on three new forms. First, *aggregation across time*, in that a small problem today can become a big problem tomorrow. The Taliban, for example, was fostered by the United States as an expedient means to stabilise Afghanistan, but later went on to support Al Qaeda attacks against Western targets. Second, *aggregation across space*, in that an event in one part of the world can quickly cascade to others. Cartoons negatively portraying the Muslim Prophet Muhammad, published in Denmark in 2005, caused shockwaves and violence throughout much of the Middle East and the broader Muslim world, where the cartoons were seen as blasphemous. And third, *aggregation across scale*, in that a problem that afflicts individuals can increasingly afflict societies. Individual drug consumption may lead to large scale drug consumption, and, in turn, a demand for drug trafficking across a whole region.

Due to this aggregation, many have pointed out the need to expand the concept of national security—which now focusses primarily on the integrity of the state—to encompass *human* security, which argues that a people-centred view of security is necessary for national, regional and global stability.[331] Indeed, threats to human security can easily and quickly aggregate to threats against the state.

Moreover, because a great number of disciplinary issues—environmental, governmental, technological, etc—can aggregate to threaten the state, they are, and should be, *securitised*, understood and treated as security issues. Moreover, as the aperture for viewing national security threats broadens, exploration of the *interactivity* of various trends, events, and other contingencies is necessary; particularly because many of these threats come with great opportunities which must not be neglected in policy formulation.

An Evolutionary Systems View of National Security

In the light of the increasing complexity of global and local affairs, an evolutionary view of national security itself must also follow suit.

A Systems View

The instruments of national security management have long been thought of as defence-oriented in nature. Police, intelligence, military, and paramilitary forces were and are central tools in successful national security strategy. However, with the possibility for security threats to emerge from multiple sources—civil society, governance, science, economics, technology, environment, politics, resources, healthcare, to name but a few—such a narrow view of security is insufficient in this emerging era.

National defence must give way to a conceptualisation of national *security*, and the military tools for managing security threats must give way to more encompassing tools of *governance*.

The interlinkages among phenomena at municipal, state, national, and international levels necessitate a shift away from jurisdiction-based management towards one based on whole systems. Diverse phenomena can have security implications for various levels of society; attempts to view them in isolation or without giving due weightage to their broader context would be counter-productive. Due to the vastly networked organisation of agents and indeed of systems, single systems can have far-reaching effects on one another.

Rather than merely articulating a set of prioritised threats in need of attention, a comprehensive understanding of *national security* today means we must view the world as a complex, evolving *system of systems*. Therein, national *strategy* must align perceived threats and opportunities from multiple sources with capacities from multiple sources.[332]

Evolutionary Perspectives: Stability and Change

As threats adapt, evolve, and emerge, so too must the means of conceptualising and responding to them. Security has long been understood as an effort to reinforce the "integrity" of the state.[333] This has, in turn, been equated, in many respects, with preservation of the status quo. Stability is indeed an important goal in an era of uncertainty. But stability should not be equated with inertia. It would be dangerous to neglect and not adapt with the evolution of the systems with which security structures have to contend, and to remain static in an environment of fluctuation.

"For an evolutionary system, *continuing development* is needed in order to maintain its fitness relative to the systems it is co-evolving with",[334] wrote the evolutionary biologist Leigh van Halen . This holds equally true for national security, its conception and a strategy that emerges from it. Conceptions of security must keep evolving with the ever-fluctuating challenges of the dynamic systems in its purview.

Many have debated the differences between "status quo" powers—those that benefit from and seek to maintain the status quo—and "revisionist" powers—revolutionary agents that seek to alter the existing order. While the former seek *security* and *stability* in order to *preserve* the status quo, the latter seek what they view as *justice*, a break in the status quo that would satisfy their demands.

The state is more often the principal that seeks security, while those that challenge the state are those that seek some form of justice. These bifurcations—security and justice, status quo and revision, even state and nation—have long been thought of as diametrically opposed to each other. But, in democracies, the notion that the state is always correct and that demands for justice are unmerited—and to believe that the state can *control* change and resist influences upon it—is simply arrogance.[335]

Moreover, the very notion of *stability*, political and otherwise, takes on a new meaning in an era typified by change and interactivity. The paradoxes of globalisation—integration and fragmentation, centralisation and decentralisation, nationalism and sub-nationalism, etc—demonstrate that change is constant, occurring simultaneously under structures of apparent stability.

An evolutionary conception of security that embraces change, the often dynamic, legitimate demands for justice, as well as the safety of a cohesive nation, reinforced by the effective apparatuses of the state, is the need of the moment This is not to say that the state should capitulate to any challenge to the status quo, but that it must address legitimate grievances while managing legitimate threats, assessing and embracing those elements of change that can be beneficial in the long-term.

With change and anomalies being the norm and interlinkages increasing on all levels of society, the future has become nearly impossible to predict. India's philosophical heritage is particularly structured to embrace these complex challenges. The legacy of *dharmic* thought sees history not as messianic and linear but as *karmic*, i.e. through networks of non-linear causality in which future events and happenings are unpredictable. Moreover, this legacy is non-Manichean, recognising that many complexities inform and create existence, rather than viewing reality as a struggle between an objectively defined good and evil. It is a view that is already in tune with an era of non-linearity, unpredictability, complexity—a view that accepts the changing nature of systems and takes into consideration a wide array of contributing factors.

However, *reflexivity* is central even to such a necessarily systemic understanding –that is to say that agents' actions *define* and create the system with which it interacts. *Dharmic* philosophy does not neglect reflexivity: one's *svadharma*, or duty within the broader evolution of history, must be recognised. Thereafter, it is upon the individual to *realise* her or his own full potential within the broader system, simultaneously *creating* and defining the contours of the system itself. In an era of multiple challenges and multiple consequences, India's position vis-à-vis the challenges it faces must be proactively and definitively shaped.

Foresight and Action

Anticipatory Governance

Linear models have defined governance to date: the future is seen as a simple extension of the past. Government today is organised to deal with the same problems as yesterday, and tomorrow's problems are expected to be the same as those of today.

As the rate of the aggregation of events increases, future scenarios, including threats become increasingly unpredictable. The systems of threats that India faces are inherently *non-linear*; a small event in one part of a system may have large consequences for the whole, while a large event may have disproportionately small effects, all depending on which other variables come into play. Quite naturally, threats too are non-linear, non-sequential and, thus, un*predict*able.

Linear attempts to predict the future are incomplete at best and give a false sense of omniscience. Instead, challenges must be *anticipated* by understanding the drivers, trends, potential events, and weak signals—anomalous entities that may become pervasive—that may shape the emerging strategic environment.

Thus, tied to the notion of national *strategy*, and in particular national security strategy, India should take a page from the book of the Government of Singapore's Risk Assessment and Horizon Scanning Group (RAHS):

> [It]coordinates a Government-wide network comprising 20 agencies covering strategic and operational counterterrorism, environmental scanning and scenario planning, biomedical surveillance, cyber surveillance, maritime security, chemical-biological-radiological explosives surveillance, energy security and education. [It] aims to *identify early on threats and opportunities, the early indicators that could have an impact* on Singapore… [It uses] weak signals as the starting point and the agencies [say what is] relevant.[336]

India must anticipate different scenarios, contingencies, trends, and events, and engage the relevant domestic and global actors sooner rather than later as it maximises the benefits and minimises the costs of each. Strategic surprise, while taking on a new meaning in the light of the constant evolution of global systems, should no longer be viable.

Diverse Thinking

As global affairs become increasingly anomalous and threats emerge from various sources, the *possibilities* of systems become more important than their limitations. And because threats emerge from the interaction and aggregation of many drivers, anticipating these threats and their manifestations requires increasingly *creative* thinking.

As Dr. Yaneer Bar-Yam of the New England Complex Systems Institute writes: "The essence of creativity [is] creating new possibilities out of combinations of what already exists…a process of putting old parts together in new ways."[337] Links between otherwise disparate areas allow knowledge and information to flow, allowing new combinations to form and emerge as innovative ideas and change.

Strategic thinking, planning, and policy-making must be informed by *diverse* groups of thinkers in order to generate more creative analyses. Diversity is important because, as Gompert, et al., put it,

> ...the errors of individuals tend to cancel out one another as numbers increase, leaving the average to be that much better…Moreover, the full range of experiences, perspectives, and information of the many are

in play, resulting in a better answer than if the solution is based on the experience, perspectives, and information of only a few, even if they are of above average intelligence.[338]

A wise step taken to bring about this diversity was the establishment in 1998 of the National Security Council (NSC) to comprehensively assess India's political, economic, energy and strategic security concerns. This was done by bringing together the inter-disciplinary Strategic Policy Group; the Joint Intelligence Committee (JIC) or National Security Council Secretariat (NSCS) to aggregate and analyse information; and the National Security Advisory Board (NSAB), consisting of 30 persons outside the government, to assess long-term contingencies.[339] There have been many hiccups since its inception, and doubts about the body's efficacy abound, but that is to be expected of any young government agency.[340]

A structure that integrates various facets of security, diverse knowledge and experience—including perspectives from outside the government—is seminal for forward and creative thinking. "Collective wisdom only works if there is ample diversity and independence of views among the participants… [in the absence of] diversity and independence, 'groupthink'—the foe of reason—may emerge."[341] The processes of the body, and the way it is managed, however, must be altered to make it more effective for its allotted task. The lack of a change management strategy to oversee the agency's development and ensure effective processes over time was perhaps the agency's initial stumbling block.

Networked Management

The resolution of problems, particularly in an era of finite resources, requires multi-pronged solutions that simultaneously tackle various dimensions of interconnected problems. Again, due to aggregation, single issues require different *scales* and *angles* of address; geographic, disciplinary, and jurisdictional boundaries can no longer dictate response. Stove-piped, hierarchical solutions are not appropriate for problems that do not easily fit into boxes. Networked solutions to networked problems require *networked management*.

The NSC, as a body for coordinating policy and enabling links between otherwise stove-piped jurisdictions, would ideally allow knowledge and information to flow laterally at upper echelons.

But beyond influencing strategic planning, integration of different bureaucracies must be enabled and encouraged at the *operational* level. Rapid communication and coordination between disciplines are necessary when dealing with complex problems. By enabling creativity and *flexibility* through enhanced connectivity, networked management uses the existing knowledge and processes of existing institutions—without creating new bureaucracies—to proactively pool and coordinate resources that already exist in different parts of government.

While inter-disciplinary thinking is slowly coming to the fore in policy management, there is no concerted, protracted method of cross-*scale* governance. 'Multi-scale' networked management—a hybrid of top-down hierarchy and laterally connected networks—across scales, jurisdiction and discipline must enable agencies to communicate and coordinate directly with agencies and jurisdictions across cities, states, and governments around the country and the world.

Control Structures

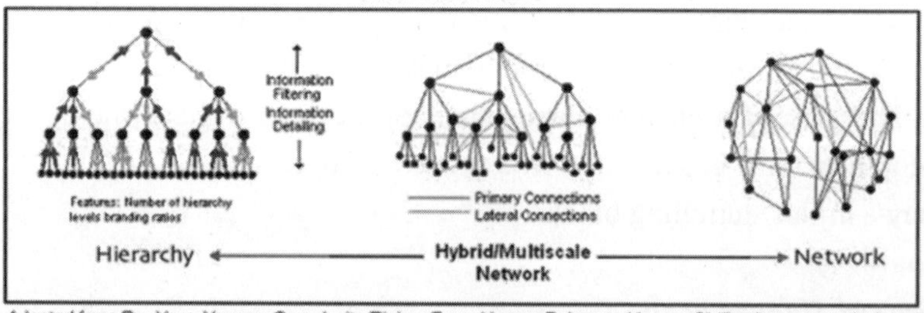

Adapted from Bar-Yam, Yaneer, Complexity Rising: From Human Beings to Human Civilization, a complexity profile

Though such practices would circumvent traditional, hierarchical and federalised systems, they are necessary for sufficiently flexible, coordinated, and creative governance.

A prime example of the inefficacy of unconnected, stove-piped management would be within India's federal defence branches. The way the local police force, the national Army, national paramilitary forces (including those with counter-insurgency and anti-terrorist missions) and intelligence apparatuses are organised is jurisdictionally and geographically stove-piped, with minimal lateral connectivity between them. For example, during the terrorist attacks on Mumbai, Maharashtra, on November 26, 2008, National Security Guard (NSG) commandos had to be flown into Mumbai from their base in Manesar, Haryana, delaying response time and compromising the counter-terror mission considerably.[342] Likewise, in the aftermath of large-scale incidents—terrorist, bombings, riots, and so forth—including 26/11, national intelligence agencies and local police are in the habit of blaming one another for insufficient communication regarding the threat.

If there was cross-pollination of agencies –for example, if the expertise and capacities from paramilitary forces were integrated into local police forces, or if a Research and Analysis Wing (R&AW) desk was established in a central Mumbai Police Thana—such deficits of, and delays in, communication and action that aided the adversary would not exist.

The same case for networking can be made at the societal level. The small number of minority communities' members —particularly Muslims— in the Indian Army, Police and Paramilitary Forces is an issue that has been widely discussed in academia and media. As a result of this deficit, there is a great deal of distrust between the forces and minority communities, a lack of communication of information between the government and society (a weak state-nation relationship), and, very often, communalisation of the forces that results in excessive violence.[343] To solve this problem, enhanced integration between the government and minority communities is necessary; as Shashi Tharoor articulates:

> [Minority populations] ...need to feel the police is part of them, rather than an external entity...we need to enhance the recruitment and retention of minorities in the police forces and to conduct police outreach to minority communities. Such an approach would simultaneously reduce a major source of grievance in the Muslim community, increase the trust between the police and the people they are policing, and dramatically improve our own intelligence about currents within a community whose vulnerability to the blandishments of terror is high.[344]

The New York Police Department (NYPD) has practised inter-community networking of this sort effectively, recruiting police officers and intelligence analysts from various minority communities in its diverse polity. In addition to providing linguistic and cultural skills and community access, minority communities have also contributed to the NYPD's strategic thinking. Italian Americans in New York assisted in the crackdown on the *Cosa Nostra* Mafia, while Muslim-Americans have contributed to the NYPD's counter-terrorism strategy.[345]

Moreover, in seeking to address some of the failures of governance discussed—namely, systemic corruption—institutionalised lateral connections (networks) may play a pivotal role in providing accountability as well. In part due to high levels of bureaucratic red tape that retard governance processes, informal networks have emerged to expedite these processes, many of which circumvent official processes and even encourage corruption. As journalist Suketu Mehta writes, in countries like India, "you need to pull strings to do the simplest things: get a train reservation or a government document. You must know someone. There's very little you can do anonymously, as a member of the vast masses."[346]

As a result, unofficial processes and informal networks *already* typify the administration of much social provision in India—informal networks, in fact, become the *de facto* processes of governance. Management experts such as Ralph Stacey argue that it is these 'naturally' occurring networks that should be the focus of any organisational or governance reforms,[347] as they are the sources of "diversity of thought approach" and are "often the place where much of the creativity resides within the organization, as it...has few rules and constraints."[348] Fundamentally, networks are how governance systems already work, and should be understood, engaged, and capitalised upon when bringing about institutional reforms.[349]

This is particularly pertinent as top-down approaches to check corruption and inefficiencies in governance have proved ineffective in the past. Increasing reliance on networks and lateral connections, by greater interaction *across* organisations, raises the level of *competitiveness* within an organisation. Coupled with the cooperation generally mandated by vertically organised hierarchies, competition can bring about a greater degree of efficiency within governance.

Lower-level integration may require change-management strategies that consider physical alterations—i.e. modified government architecture; a shift to greater reliance on information and communication technologies that have decentralised processes in business[350] and social organisation[351] ; and inculcating organisational cultures that encourage interaction.

Fundamentally, networked organisation is a must for managing the increasingly complex challenges to governance.

Conclusion

As the level of interactivity in the world increases, the challenges that India faces at the micro level, macro level and the scale between to two, will become increasingly complex. A whole-scale reform of governance is necessary if India is to effectively address the myriad challenges it faces. Such a reform must engage key individuals from federal, state and municipal government bodies; academia and private sector organisations; the leadership of all political parties and key bureaucrats and; most importantly, the civil society, so as to create the necessary political will to and ensure democratic overview of the process. As argued in an earlier article,

> Once and for all, there should be a comprehensive, multi-partisan effort to overhaul governance—particularly of national security—devoid of politicking and replete with citizen overview . Security threats today and into the future will emerge constantly and from multiple sources...What is needed are networked intelligence and anticipatory governance that transcend geographic and jurisdictional boundaries – a reformed system would capitalize on India's strengths: software, broad-scale engagement and diversity of thought. India must carry out a thorough review, revision, and an overhaul of its national security system, in which discussions and reports turn into concrete action and reform.[352]

In a governance system as expansive as India's, such a task may appear particularly ambitious. Indeed, it is. But in the light of the plethora of emerging, evolving security threats that India faces, nothing less than an ambitious overhaul is needed. Moreover, such efforts, however flawless in execution, may never be 100 per cent successful the first time around. But *any* progress in India's systems of governance is vital, and should be undergirded by an orientation towards efficiency, transparency, an evolving understanding of security and strategy, anticipatory governance and integrated systems.

India's greatest strengths lie in its diversity of culture and perspective, adaptability and flexibility, broad-scale democratic engagement and human capital. These are virtues that India must harness for a future that is India's alone to *create*.

Notes

Introduction

1. 'Fragmegration' is a portmanteau that "captures the tensions between the fragmenting and integrating forces that sustain world affairs," James N. Rosenau, "'Fragmegrative' Challenges to National Security," in Terry L. Heyns (ed), *Understanding U.S. Strategy: A Reader* (Washington, D.C.: National Defense University, 1983), pp. 65-82; and James N. Rosenau, *Along the Domestic-Foreign Frontier: Exploring Governance in a Turbulent World* (Cambridge: Cambridge University Press, 1997), ch. 6.
2. See, for example, Barry Wellman, "Little Boxes, Glocalization, and Networked Individualism," in Makoto Tanabe et al (eds), *Digital Cities II* (Berlin: Springer-Verlag, 2002), pp. 11-25.
3. Manuel Castells, *The Rise of the Network Society, The Information Age: Economy, Society and Culture Vol. I* (Cambridge, MA; Oxford, UK: Blackwell, 1996).
4. Leon Fuerth, "Strategic Myopia," *The National Interest*, March 1, 2006.
5. James Rosenau, "Many Damn Things Simultaneously: Complexity Theory and World Affairs," Paper presented at the Conference on Complexity, Global Politics, and National Security, sponsored by the National Defense University and the RAND Corporation, Washington, D.C., November 13, 1996.
6. This 'trifurcation' of global systems is a theoretical construct put forth by James Rosenau, *Distant Proximities: Dynamics Beyond Globalization* (Princeton: Princeton University Press, 2003); and earlier, James Rosenau, *Turbulence in World Politics: A Theory of Change and Continuity* (Princeton: Princeton University Press, 1990).

Micro Level Challenges

7. See, for example Castells, 1996, op. cit.
8. Government refers to management of the commons steeped in highly formalised legal procedures mandated by official processes, while govern*ance* is the way in which rule systems are marked by both formal and informal procedures, James Rosenau, "Globalization and Governance: Bleak Prospects for Stability," in James

Rosenau, Ernst-Ulrich von Weizsacker and Ulrich Petschow (eds), *Governance and Sustainability: Exploring the Roadmap to Sustainability after Johannesburg* (Sheffield: Greenleaf Publising, 2004).

9. 'Control' of information refers to its contextualisation, processing, and framing.
10. The term 'security dilemma' was popularised by John H. Herz in his *Political Realism and Political Idealism: A Study in Theories and Realities* (Chicago: University of Chicago Press, 1951).
11. Ashutosh Varshney, *Ethnic Conflict and Civic Life: Hindus and Muslims in India* (New Haven: Yale University Press, 2003).
12. For an analysis of this bifurcation as applied to Hindu-Muslim rivalry in India, see, for example, David Ludden (ed), *Making India Hindu* (Oxford University Press, 1996).
13. Samuel P. Huntington, "The Clash of Civilizations?", *Foreign Affairs*, Summer, 1993.
14. Similar theories regarding the incompatibility and eventual conflict between religious communities in India in particular had been put forth on multiple occasions prior to Huntington's own 1993 articulation. The most prominent of these is the *Two-Nation Theory* that served as the basis for the partition of the subcontinent. The Two-Nation Theory argued that Muslims and Hindus were fundamentally two different nations and peoples so divergent in customs, lifestyles, and beliefs that they would not be able to peaceably occupy the same land. The theory had early proponents amongst such persons as 11th century Persian Scholar Abu Rayhan al-Biruni, Sayyed Ahmed Khan, the Muslim League's Muhammad Ali Jinnah, and Hindutva ideologue Vinayak Damodar Savarkar.
15. The following analogies are only for example, and are not based on any specific case.
16. Amartya Sen, "What Clash of Civilizations? Why Religious Identity isn't Destiny", *The Slate*, March 29, 2006, adapted from Amartya Sen, *Identity and Violence: The Illusion of Destiny* (Norton and Company, 2006).
17. The history of the Balkans, and the very term "Balkanisation" is a strong case in point. For decades, 'Yugoslavian' identity was sufficient to tie the people of the region together socially and politically. Following that, 'Yugoslavian' identity was broken into the collective identity of 'Serbians,' who were defined against 'Croats'. 'Serbians' were fragmented further into 'Kosovars' and 'Albanians.' Geographic and political division followed all of these shifts in identity; and the prospect for further fragmentation certainly remains. See, for example, Maria Todorova, *Imagining the Balkans* (Oxford University Press, 2009); for theoretical expositions of the concept, see, for example, Michael Zwerin, *A Case for the Balkanization of Practically Everyone: The New Nationalism* (Wildwood House, 1976); and Dusan

Bjelic and Obrad Savic (eds), *Balkan as Metaphor: Between Globalization and Fragmentation* (The MIT Press, 2005).

18. John Arquilla and David Ronfeldt, "The Advent of Netwar (Revisited)," in John Arquilla and David Ronfeldt, *Networks and Netwars: The Future of Terror, Crime, and Militancy* (RAND Corporation, 2001).
19. For example, the rise of the Bharatiya Janata Party (BJP)—a party that, in its political discourse, espoused a more aggressive brand of Hinduism to the detriment of non-Hindu minorities—*through the democratic system* may have tarnished otherwise positive views of the system itself amongst many minorities.
20. William M. Evan, "An Organization-Set Model of Interorganizational Relations," in Matthew Tuite, Roger Chisholm, and Michael Radnor (eds), *Interorganizational Decisionmaking* (Chicago: Aldine Publishing Company, 1972), pp. 181–200; See also Arquilla and Ronfeldt, 2001, op. cit.
21. Duncan J. Watts and Steven Strogatz, "Collective Dynamics of 'Small-World' Networks", *Nature*, June 1998.
22. Mark Granovetter, "The Strength of Weak Ties: A Network Theory Revisited", *Sociology Theory*, Vol. 1, 1983, pp. 201-233.
23. See, for example, Sushil Bikhchandani, David Hirshleifer, and Ivo Welch, "A Theory of Fads, Fashion, Custom, and Cultural Change as Informational Cascades", *Journal of Political Economy*, Vol. 100, No.5, 1992, pp. 992-1026.
24. Sean J. A. Edwards, *Swarming on the Battlefield: Past, Present, and Future* (RAND Corporation, 2000), available at http://www.rand.org/pubs/monograph_reports/MR1100/, accessed November 12, 2008.
25. Phil Williams, "Transnational Criminal Networks", in Arquilla and Ronfeldt, 2001, op. cit.
26. Jessica T. Matthews, "Power Shift", *Foreign Affairs*, January/February 1997, pp. 53.
27. Howard Reingold, *Smart Mobs: The Next Social Revolution* (Basic Books, 2002).
28. Clive Thompson, "The Year in Ideas: Smart Mobs", *New York Times,* December 12, 2002.
29. "The political effects can be astonishing. In the Philippines last year, smart mobs helped topple President Joseph Estrada. Barely an hour after fresh news of corruption arose, a text message forwarded from citizen to citizen ("Go 2EDSA, Wear black") summoned thousands of black-clad protesters to a public plaza. In America, anti-globalisation advocates now use text messages to avoid the police at demonstrations; groups split up and reform like amoebas. This process isn't always so benign; mobs can be about lynching as often as democracy. Last month's Miss World eruption in Nigeria was triggered partly by texting: angry Muslims used their phones to pass on news of an article praising the pageant. Within days, more

than 200 people had been killed." Clive Thompson, "The Year in Ideas: Smart Mobs", *New York Times,* December 12, 2002.

30. A great deal of the material on 'networks' is based on the author's own studies over the last years, and specific citations would be difficult to render. For primers on network theory, see, for example, Duncan Watts, *Six Degrees: The Science of a Connected Age* (W. W. Norton & Company, 2003); Albert-László Barabási, *Linked: How Everything Is Connected to Everything Else* (Plume Press, 2002); and Mark Buchanan, *Nexus: Small Worlds and the Groundbreaking Theory of Networks* (W.W. Norton & Company, 2003). For specific material on social network analysis, the material in this forthcoming section, see, for example, Karen Stephenson, *Quantum Theory of Trust* (Pearson Press, 2006); Robert L. Cross and Andrew Parker, *The Hidden Power of Social Networks: Understanding How Work Really Gets Done in Organizations* (Harvard Business School Press, 2004).
31. Alternate definitions of 'insurgency' include "an internal conflict in which (1) a group or groups are trying to overthrow the government or secede from it; (2) more than 1,000 have died over the course of the war; and (3) more than 100 have died on each side," Seth G. Jones and Martin Libicki, *How Terrorist Groups End: Lessons for Countering al Qa'ida* (RAND Corporation, 2008); or "A political-military campaign by nonstate actors seeking to overthrow a government or secede from a country through the use of unconventional—and, sometimes, conventional—military strategies and tactics," US Joint Chiefs of Staff, *Department of Defense Dictionary of Military and Associated Terms*, Washington, D.C., joint publication 1-02, ongoing since 1972, p. 266.
32. Many, for example, credit the cessation of Khalistani terrorism in Punjab with a hard-handed approach by the then Directors-General of Police; see for example K.P.S. Gill, *Punjab: Knights of Falsehood* (Har Anand Publications, 1997). This common view ascribing the end of terrorism and insurgency in Punjab to a hard-handed approach, however, also neglects certain economic factors that may have contributed to political changes in the region. Increasing development in neighbouring states—particularly those that fed the migration to Punjab that stressed resources and capacities in that region—reduced the impetus for migration to Punjab, freeing local capacities there and diminishing the economic grievances that may have moved many Punjabis to violence.
33. Jones and Libicki, 2008, op. cit.
34. See, for example, Joel Garreau, "Disconnect the Dots: Maybe We Can't Cut off Terror's Head, but we can Take out its Nodes", *Washington Post*, September 17, 2001.
35. See, for example, Jason Burke, *Al Qaeda: Casting a Shadow of Terror* (IB Tauris, 2003).

36. Brian A. Jackson et al, *Aptitude for Destruction: Organizational Learning in Terrorist Groups and Its Implications for Combating Terrorism* (RAND Corporation, 2005), pp. xi-xii.
37. See, for example, Robert Pape, *Dying to Win: The Strategic Logic of Suicide Terrorism* (Random House, 2005), p. 104.
38. The case demonstrated is exaggerated for the sake of example. For the specifics on Al Qaeda's post-9/11 adaptation see, for example, Rohan Gunaratna, *Inside Al Qaeda: Global Network of Terror* (Berkeley Publishing Group, 2003).
39. Thinkers such as Bruce Hoffman and Anatol Lieven have argued that "it is Al Qaeda policy to stage terrorist incidents in the West so that Western governments [and populations] turn on Muslims, which will eventually radicalize the latter, bringing them on the same ideological wavelength as the organization that Osama Bin Laden heads." See Khalid Hasan, "Al Qaeda wants to Radicalize Western Governments", *Daily Times*, April 2, 2006.
40. Paul Brass, *The Production of Hindu-Muslim Violence in Contemporary India* (Washington, DC: University of Washington Press, 2003).
41. This is the case when defining the 'black economy' as all economic activities that are not officially registered by the government Arun Kumar, *The Black Economy in India* (Penguin Books India, 1999).
42. Kumar, Ibid., p. 26.
43. Looney, 2002, op. cit.
44. Gunaratna, 2003, op. cit.
45. Shankar Pratap Singh, "Transnational Organized Crime: The Indian Perspective," in Kunihiki Sakai, Work Product of the 119th International Training Session, Current Situation of and Countermeasures against Transnational Organised Crime, UNAFEI, Japan, October 2002, pp. 572-573.
46. Atul Aneja, "Where Big can be Bothersome", *The Hindu*, January 7, 2001.
47. Gunaratna, 2003, op. cit., p. 221.
48. *London Times*, May 1993, cited in Pratap Singh, 2002, op. cit., pp. 572-573.
49. *Over a Barrel: Light Weapons and Human Rights in the Commonwealth,* Commonwealth Human Rights Initiative, 1999.
50. Bhavna Bij-Aurora, "Blazing Saddles: Half the World's Small Arms Supply, 40 Million guns, Wreaks Havoc in the Countryside", *Outlook India*, April 3, 2006.
51. P.V. Ramana, "The Maoist Web: An Overview," in P.V. Ramana (ed), *The Naxal Challenge: Causes, Linkages, and Policy Options* (New Delhi: Pearson-Longman, 2008), ch. 10.
52. See, for example, Wasbir Hussein, "Insurgency in India's Northeast Cross-Border Links and Strategic Alliances", *Faultlines*, Vol. 17, February 2006; Sultan Shahin, "Pakistan Shifts Proxy War to India's East", *Asia Times*, February 6, 2002; Peter

Chalk, "Pakistan's Role in the Kashmir Insurgency", *Jane's Intelligence Review*, September 1, 2001; Manu Pubby, "China Emerging as Main Source of Arms to N-E Rebels: Jane's Review", *Indian Express*, May 21, 2008.

53. See, for example, Indrani Bagchi, "Insurgent Groups in NE Getting Help from China?", *Times of India*, October 31, 2008; and Sarah Meek, "Light Weapons and Early Warning: Initial Steps", in P. Cross (ed), *Contributing to Preventive Action, Conflict Prevention Network Yearbook 97/98* (Brussels: Stiftung Wissenschaft und Politik, 1998), ch. 7.
54. Pratap Singh, 2002, op. cit.
55. An internationally acknowledged legal challenge, however, is that of distinguishing between human smuggling, that which is for consensual purposes of employment and often manipulated thereafter, and human trafficking, for forced labour, employment, and sex.
56. Pratap Singh, 2002, op. cit.
57. Ibid.
58. Neeraj Kumar, "Organized Crime," *India Seminar*, No. 482, November 1999.
59. Flooding Indian markets with counterfeit rupees in order to artificially drive up inflation has been a key tactic of the Pakistani Inter-Services Intelligence agency, which has used organised crime syndicates and their agents as instruments of such practices. See, for example, Suketu Mehta, *Maximum City: Bombay Lost and Found* (Alfred A. Knopf Press, 2004).
60. See, for example, Subha Chandran, "Terrorism and Organized Crime in India," Institute for Peace and Conflict Studies, Article No. 973, February 23, 2003.
61. The dynamic organisational tactics of terrorism, for example, are a similar analogue: while Al Qaeda once served as the central hub of Islamist terrorism, connecting various 'spokes'—local terrorist groups—increasingly, these local groups have begun to coordinate with one another directly, without having to go through a central authority. What was once a more centralised 'star-hub' network has become a distributed, decentralised, highly connected 'all-channel' network.
62. Take, for example, the case of Kerala, where a consumption-based economy is "propped up by $5.5 billion annual remittances from 3.5m Keralites who work abroad, 85% of them in the Middle East." "Defiantly Poor", *The Economist*, April 22, 2006.
63. Amit Gupta, "The Indian Diaspora's Political Efforts in the United States", *ORF Occasional Paper*, September 2004, available at http://www.observerindia.com/cms/export/orfonline/modules/occasionalpaper/attachments/op040918_1163398084234.pdf, accessed December 19, 2008.
64. See, for example, Anjana Chatterji, "US-Based Hindus Funding Indian Terrorism - A Report Indian Diaspora Funding Hindu Extremism", *Daily Times,* Wednesday,

July 31, 2002.

65. See, for example, Rohan Gunaratna, *Sri Lanka's Ethnic Conflict and National Security* (Colombo: South Asian Network on Conflict Research, 1998).
66. See, for example, Simrat Dhillonn, "The Sikh Diaspora and the Quest for Khalistan: A Search for Statehood or for Self-Preservation", *IPCS Research Paper*, December 2007; and Giorgio Shani, "Beyond Khalistan? Sikh Diasporic Identity and Critical International Theory", *Sikh Formulations*, Vol. 1, No. 1, June 2005, pp. 57-74.
67. See, for example, J. Millard Burr and Robert O. Collins, *Alms for Jihad: Charity and Terrorism in the Islamic World* (Cambridge University Press, 2006).
68. "Clouds over Council of Khalistan and Burton", *India Abroad*, April 25, 1997.
69. Daniel Byman, et al, *Trends in Outside Support for Insurgent Movements* (RAND Corporation, 2001).
70. The 'international,' bilateral, and diplomatic angles of this issue are discussed in the next section
71. "Unfit for Service", *The Economist*, January 17, 2008.
72. Personal interview with Julius Ribeiro, former Director-General of Police for Punjab and Maharashtra, October 29, 2008.
73. David Gompert, Irving Lachow, and Justin Perkins, *Battle-Wise: Seeking Time-Information Superiority in Networked Warfare* (Centre for Technology and National Security Policy, National Defense University Press, 2006).
74. Major General Satbir Singh, "Measures to Attract and Retain Talent in the Indian Army", CLAWS, Article No. 1170, September 5, 2008, available at http://clawsindia.in/index.php?action=master&task=171&u_id=43
75. "Unfit for Service", *The Economist*, January 17, 2008. A deficit in personnel also affects other sectors of the Indian government, namely, the legal and judicial systems. A deficit of judges at various levels of the legal system throughout the country leaves long backlogs of cases that number in the thousands. See, for example, Ashwini Kumar Bansal, "Burden of Backlog: Towards Speedy Dispensation of Justice", *Tribune India*, May 20, 2007.
76. Privatisation refers to the "exit of the government as a producer in a given market, and complete transfer of the government ownership to the private player," Parashar Kulkarni, "Liberalization/Privatization in India: Disinvestment Revenue and Market Structures," Centre for Civil Society, 2003, available at http://www.ccs.in/ccsindia/ec/ec_parashar.pdf, accessed December 22, 2008
77. Disinvestment refers to the "reduction in government equity in public sector enterprises," Kulkarni, 2003, op. cit.
78. See, for example, Ajay Shah, "How Important is Privatization in India?", *Business Standard*, March 21, 2007; Vikram Khanna, "Interview with Arun Shourie, India's Minister for Disinvestment," *The Business Times*, April 10, 2002.

79. Saritha Rai, "Fraud Reports Worry India Outsourcing Firms", *International Herald Tribune*, October 5, 2006; Ed Frauenhaim, "Insecurities Over Indian Outsourcing", *CNET News*, April 26, 2005.
80. Shantanu Chakrabarti, "Private Security Firms for Internal Security: An Idea Whose Time has Come", *South Asia Monitor*, June 26, 2008, available at http://www.southasiamonitor.org/2008/June/news/26wsa1.shtml, accessed December 24, 2008.
81. See, for example, Joanna Abrisketa, "Blackwater: Mercenaries and International Law", *FRIDE: Comment*, October 2007, available at http://www.fride.org/download/blackwater.english.pdf, accessed January 14, 2009.
82. John Broder and James Risen, "Blackwater Tops Firms in Iraq in Shooting Rate", *New York Times*, September 27, 2007.
83. In the case of the private security firm Blackwater, employed in US operations in Iraq, Blackwater has faced criminal charges in its killings of Iraqi civilians, a high-profile issue that served as a major political, diplomatic, and strategic setback to US operations in that country. See, for example, James Glanz and Sabrina Tavernise, "Security Firm Faces Criminal Charges in Iraq", *New York Times*, September 23, 2007; Jeremy Scahill, *Blackwater: The Rise of the World's Most Powerful Mercenary Army* (Nation Books, 2008); James Glanz and Sabrina Tavernise, "Security Firm Faces Criminal Charges in Iraq", *New York Times*, September 23, 2007.
84. Sean Creehan, "Soldiers of Fortune 500 International Mercenaries", *Harvard International Review*, Winter 2002.
85. Mehta, 2004, op. cit.
86. "Cycle of Killings in Kashmir Fuels Conflict", Human Rights Watch, July 1, 1999; "India's Secret Army in Kashmir: New Patterns of Abuse Emerge in the Conflict", A Human Rights Watch Report, May 1996, Vol. 8, No. 4 (C)
87. "Civil society activists in Manipur say that while some militants might be in the business of making money, most are fighting for independence in a cycle of violence that has been fueled, at least in part, by decades of government neglect and corruption and human rights violations by Indian security forces," "These Fellows Must Be Eliminated: Relentless Violence and Impunity in Manipur," A Human Rights Watch Report, September 2008.
88. Saba Naqvi, "Few Blind Men Of Hindostan: Why is the Indian State Quick to Nail Minority Offences but Myopic to Sangh Transgressions?", *Outlook India*, October 6, 2008.
89. "We Have no Orders to Save You: State Participation and Complicity in Communal Violence in Gujarat," A Human Rights Watch Report, April 2002, Vol. 14, No. 3 (C).

90. Justice B. N. Srikrishna, *Full Report of the Justice B. N. Srikrishna Commission on the Mumbai Riots of 1992–1993* (Sabrang Publishers, 2001).
91. Personal interview with Julio Ribeiro, former Director-General of Police, Punjab and Maharashtra, October 29, 2008.
92. Yaneer Bar-Yam, *Making Things Work: Solving Complex Problems in a Complex World* (Knowledge Press, 2004).
93. John Arquilla, for example, argues that networked threats must be dealt with by networked responses, see Arquilla and Ronfeldt, 2001, op. cit.
94. See, for example, "Rivalry Between Intelligence Agencies is Costing India Lives", *IANS*, December 10, 2008.
95. This metaphor was conceived independently by the author, but the term 'flailing' was employed and expanded by Lant Pritchett in his unpublished essay, "Is India a Flailing State? Detours on the Four Lane Highway to Modernization," Harvard University Kennedy School of Government, September 19, 2008, available at http://ksghome.harvard.edu/~lpritch/Papers/Is%20India%20a%20Flailing%20 State_v1.pdf, accessed December 14, 2008.
96. See, for example, N. Vittal, *Corruption in India: The Roadblock to National Prosperity* (Academic Foundation, 2003); K. N. Gupta, *Corruption in India* (Anmol Publications Pvt Ltd, 2001).
97. To distinguish these terms, it may be helpful to reference a piece by James Rosenau, in which 'governance' refers to rule systems are marked by both formal and informal procedures, whereas 'government' refers strictly to the highly formalised and legal procedures mandated by official processes; James Rosenau, "Globalization and Governance: Bleak Prospects for Stability," in James Rosenau, Ernst-Ulrich von Weizsacker and Ulrich Petschow (eds), *Governance and Sustainability: Exploring the Roadmap to Sustainability after Johannesburg* (Sheffield: Greenleaf Publising, 2004).
98. "The Transparency International Report of 2007, while projecting the Indian judiciary as the third most corrupt institution in the country, concluded that 77 per cent of corruption in the judicial system has been lawyer-driven," N.R. Madhava Menon, "Reforming the Legal Profession: Some Ideas", *The Hindu*, February 20, 2008.
99. Gurcharan Das, "The Next World Order", *New York Times*, January 1, 2009.

Macro Level Challenges

100. William T. Wilson, *The Dawn of the India Century: Why India is Poised to Challenge China and the United States for Global Economic Hegemony in the 21st Century* (Keystone Foundation, 2005).
101. See, for example, John H. Herz, *Political Realism and Political Idealism: A Study*

in Theories and Realities (Chicago: University of Chicago Press, 1951).

102. Samuel P. Huntington, "The Clash of Civilizations?", *Foreign Affairs*, Summer, 1993. Regarding nation-states, Huntington postulates that "at the macro-level, states from different civilizations compete for relative military and economic power, struggle over the control of international institutions and third parties, and competitively promote their particular political and religious values."
103. The way that the British media, as well as the Indian government, altered the way they framed and acted upon the Kashmir militancy issue in the wake of the 9/11 attacks and subsequent "War on Terror" is analysed in Samir Saran, "Kashmir—Representations of Terror: How has the British Press Portrayed the Militant Violence in Kashmir in the Aftermath of the 9/11 Terrorist Strikes in the US?", (Unpublished Paper, London School of Economics, 2008).
104. See, for example, Prem Shankar Jha, *Kashmir, 1947: Rival Versions of History* (Oxford University Press, 1996); Muhammad Ayub, *An Army; Its Role & Rule (A History of the Pakistan Army from Independence to Kargil 1947-1999* (Rosedog Books, 2005).
105. "When Trade Winds Smell Sweet", *The Economist*, April 10, 2008; "Opportunities for constructing win-win situations by reconciling business profitability with broader social objectives in external engagement", Panel at International Conference: Engaging with a Resurgent Africa, Conference hosted by the Observer Research Foundation and the Rose Luxembourg Foundation, November 20-21, 2008.
106. "India-Kazakhstan Engagement: Issues and Prospects," International Conference organised by the Observer Research Foundation, New Delhi, December 18-19,2008
107. Shashi Tharoor, "Making the Most of India's Soft Power", *Times of India*, January 27, 2007.
108. See, for example, "When Trade Winds Smell Sweet", *The Economist*, April 10, 2008.
109. For an exemplary neorealist analysis of the Indo-Pakistan conflict, from which this section samples, please see the comprehensive account of Rajesh Rajagopalan, "Neorealist Theory and the India-Pakistan Conflict," in Kanti Bajpai and Siddharth Mallavarapu, *International Relations in India: Theorizing the Region and Nation* (Orient Blackswan, 2005).
110. Stephen M. Walt, *The Origins of Alliances* (Ithaca: Cornell University Press, 1987), pp. 21–26.
111. The issue of the *reasons* for aggressive intentions will be taken up presently.
112. See, for example, Kenneth Waltz, *Theory of International Politics* (McGraw-Hill, 1979).
113. Rajagopalan, 2005, op. cit.

114. Ibid., p. 156.
115. Stephen Philip Cohen writes that, "because he had to weld together disparate elements of the Indian Muslim community, [Muslim League leader Muhammad Ali] Jinnah's arguments were deliberately vague. This vagueness brought both strength and weakness to the Pakistan movement, enabling it to muster support for independence and opposition to Hindu domination, but not to build a consensus on the kind of state Pakistan was to become." Stephen Philip Cohen, *The Idea of Pakistan* (Brookings Institution Press, 2004), p. 29.
116. Shuja Nawaz, *Crossed Swords: Pakistan, Its Army, and the Wars Within* (Oxford University Press, 2008), ch. 4.
117. Ayesha Siddiqa, *Military Inc.: Inside Pakistan's Military Economy* (London: Pluto Press, 2007).
118. Hussain Haqqani, "America's New Alliance with Pakistan: Avoiding the Traps of the Past", Carnegie Endowment Policy Brief, No. 19, October 2002, available at http://www.carnegieendowment.org/files/Policybrief19.pdf, accessed January 16, 2009.
119. Cohen, 2004, op. cit., p. 121.
120. For example, in her autobiography, Benazir Bhutto, the long-time head of the Pakistan People's Party, expresses the anger, humiliation, and vengefulness against India that emerged amongst both civilian and military establishments following Pakistan's dismemberment at the hand of India in the 1971 War. Benazir Bhutto, *Daughter of Destiny: An Autobiography* (Simon and Shuster, 1989).
121. See, for example, Hussain Haqqani, *Pakistan: Between Mosque and Military* (Carnegie Endowment for International Peace, 2005); Maya Chadda, "Talibinization of Pakistan's Transitional Democracy" *World Affairs*, Sept/Oct 1999.
122. See, for example, Wilson John, "Resurgent Radicalism in Pakistan: A Case Study of Jamaat ud-Dawa", Research paper for the ORF Foundation Day Seminar, September 5, 2008.
123. Zahid Hussein, *Frontline Pakistan: The Struggle with Militant Islam* (Columbia University Press, 2007); Larry Goodson, *Talibanization of Pakistan* (Palgrave Macmillan Press, 2007).
124. As George Tanham writes, "Pakistan is the villain in Indian eyes and has violated the rules for the defense of the continent. Its very creation broke up the continent's strategic unity…and Pakistan's refusal to accept India's leadership of the region, and its invitation to outsiders to support it militarily, all worked to make the breakup of the subcontinent permanent." George Tanham, "Indian Strategic Culture", The Washington Quarterly, Vol. 15, No. 1, Winter 1992
125. Hussain Haqqani, "America's New Alliance with Pakistan: Avoiding the Traps of the Past", Carnegie Endowment Policy Brief, No. 19, October 2002, available at

http://www.carnegieendowment.org/files/Policybrief19.pdf, accessed January 16, 2009.

126. Moreover, Indian analysts often assess, and the state initiates ties with, third countries based on the latter's stance on Pakistan and Indo-Pakistan relations.

127. Sundeep Waslekar et al, *The Final Settlement: Restructuring India-Pakistan Relations* (The Strategic Foresight Group, 2005).

128. Ibid.

129. See, for example, J. Mohan Malik, "India-China Relations in the 21st Century: The Continuing Rivalry", in Brahma Chellaney (ed), *Securing India's Future in the New Millennium* (Orient Blackswan, 1999).

130. David Shambaugh, "China's Identity as a Major Power," Presentation at Conference on *Worldviews of Major and Aspiring Powers: Exploring National Identities*, Elliott School of International Affairs, George Washington University, September 14, 2007.

131. Ibid. See also David Shambaugh, "China's Propaganda System: Institutions, Process & Efficacy," *The China Journal,* No. 57, January 2007.

132. This is second only to Myanmar-Thailand trade; "Sino-Myanmar Bilateral Trade up 60 Percent", *The China Post*, November 4, 2008.

133. K. Yhome, "India-Myanmar Relations (1998-2008): A Decade of Redefining Bilateral Ties", *ORF Paper*, September 19, 2008.

134. Juli MacDonald, Amy Donahue, and Bethany Danyluk, "Energy Futures in Asia", Booz Allen Hamilton Report sponsored by the Director of Net Assessment, November 2004.

135. Esther Pan, "China and Pakistan: A Deepening Bond", Council on Foreign Relations, March 8, 2006, available at http://www.cfr.org/publication/10070#2, accessed January 7, 2008.

136. As Vikram Sood, former head of India's Research and Analysis Wing, has written, "The recently inaugurated rail link from Qinghai to Lhasa is more than just a spectacular engineering marvel. It is an exhibition of Chinese determination and the rail-road will reach Xigatse near Nepal by 2010 and may be up to Kathmandu. The road infrastructure along the entire India-Tibet border has strategic implications for India in the context of an unresolved border," Vikram Sood, "Chewing Over China", *Hindustan Times*, November 13, 2006.

137. Arindam Hazare, "Colombo Port Adds to India's China Woes", *Rediff News*, October 29, 2007; Sudha Ramachandran, "China Moves into India's Backyard", *Asia Times*, March 13, 2007.

138. "Sri Lanka and the Chinese Warehouse", Strategy Page, June 2, 2007, available at http://www.strategypage.com/htmw/htproc/articles/20070602.aspx, accessed January 6, 2009; Moreover, Pakistani involvement in Sri Lankan weapons supplies

must be considered, possibly as a leg of this movement away from India

139. Christopher R. Pehrson, "String of Pearls: Meeting the Challenge of China's Rising Power Across the Asian Littoral", Strategic Studies Institute, US Army War College, July 2006, available at http://www.strategicstudiesinstitute.army.mil/pdffiles/PUB721.pdf, accessed February 19, 2009.
140. Paul Soren, "Nepal-China Military Cooperation", Observer Research Foundation, October 20, 2008.
141. A similar argument is advocated by Waslekar et al, 2005, op. cit.
142. This section was influenced heavily by Robert D. Kaplan, "Center Stage for the Twenty-First Century: Power Plays in the Indian Ocean," *Foreign Affairs*, March/April 2009.
143. Ibid.
144. Taken from the National Geospace Intelligence Agency, Coordinate Systems Analysis Branch. Map is available at http://earth-info.nga.mil/GandG/coordsys/onlinedatum/IndianOceanMap.html, accessed March 9, 2009.
145. Charles Esser, Persian Gulf Oil and Gas Exports Fact Sheet, Energy Information Administration, US Department of Energy, March 2002, available at http://www.eia.doe.gov/cabs/pgulf2.html, accessed March 12, 2009.
146. Kaplan, 2009, op. cit.
147. "Central Asia's Energy Risks", International Crisis Group, Asia Report, No. 133, May 24, 2007, available at http://www.crisisgroup.org/library/documents/asia/central_asia/133_central_asia_s_energy_risks.pdf, accessed March 8, 2009.
148. Donald Freeman, *The Straits of Malacca: Gateway or Gauntlet?,* (McGill-Queen's University Press, 2003).
149. Kaplan, 2009, op. cit.
150. Robert Kaplan has written that "one major impetus for the buildup [of the Indian Navy in the 1990s] was the humiliating inability of its navy to evacuate Indian citizens from Iraq and Kuwait during the 1990-91 Persian Gulf War." Kaplan, 2009, op. cit.
151. Alfred Thayer Mahan, *The Influence of Sea Power Upon History, 1660-1783* (Little, Brown and Company, 1890).
152. Kaplan, 2009, op. cit.
153. "Andaman Nicobar Command celebrates 4th Raising Day," Press Information Bureau, Government of India, October 7, 2005.
154. G. Parthasarathy, "India Faces Growing Chinese Hostility After 26/11", *The Hindu*, March 19, 2009.
155. R.S. Vasan, "Maritime Counter-Terrorism: An Indian Perspective," in Swati Parashar (ed), *Maritime Counter-Terrorism: A Pan-Asian Perspective* (Pearson Longman, 2008), p. 53.

156. For example, nuclear materials that have disseminated from the former Soviet Union, through the A.Q. Khan proliferation network, and potentially terrorists and pirates, while potentially linked to nation-states, often operate wholly outside of their jurisdiction. This decentralisation is, for the most part, neglected by international and multilateral endeavours, and falls on the shoulders of individual intelligence agencies.
157. "Indian Navy Foils Another Attack by Somali Pirates", *Times of India*, November 19, 2008.
158. V. Sanil Kumar, K. C. Pathak, P. Pednekar, N. S. N. Raju and R. Gowthaman, "Coastal Processes Along the Indian Coastline", *Current Science*, Vol. 91, No. 4, August 2006.
159. The Combined Task Force 150 (CTF-150), a United States Navy-led multinational naval coalition based in Djibouti, unites 15 sea-faring vessels from the US, Canada, Denmark, France, Germany, the United Kingdom, and Pakistan in an effort to police the Gulf of Aden, "Forces Combine to Train at Sea," *US Armed Forces Press Service,* January 6, 2003, available at http://www.defenselink.mil/news/Jan2003/n01062003_200301062.html, accessed February 22, 2009; See also Gal Luft and Anne Korin, "Terrorism Goes to Sea", *Foreign Affairs*, November/December 2004.
160. "There be Dragons", *The Economist*, November 6, 2008.
161. Personal interview with K. V. Kamath, CEO, ICICI Bank, in Mumbai, India, October 23, 2008.
162. "India to Continue Supporting UN Peacekeeping Operations", *India Strategic*, Vol. 3, No. 9, September 2008.
163. See, for example, Mani Shankar Aiyar, "Towards a Nuclear-Weapons-Free and Non-violent World Order", Remarks before the Conference on Pugwash, Parliamentarians and Political Will: Advancing the Agenda for Abolition, Parliamentarians for Nuclear Non-Proliferation and Disarmament, July 10–12, 2008, available at http://www.gsinstitute.org/pnnd/pubs/AIYAR_RajivGandhi.pdf, accessed January 10, 2009.
164. 1970 was the year the NPT was ratified by most signatories
165. George Perkovich, *India's Nuclear Bomb: The Impact on Global Proliferation* (University of California Press, 2001).
166. The terms of the treaty, were, of course, far more extensive. For a full version of the final document, please see http://frwebgate.access.gpo.gov/cgi-bin/getdoc.cgi?dbname=109_cong_bills&docid=f:h5682enr.txt.pdf
167. Joseph Nye, *Soft Power: The Means to Success in World Politics* (Public Affairs Press, 2004).
168. Remarks by K. Subrahmanyam, Panel Discussion and Book Release of *India's*

Nuclear Policy by Bharat Karnad, India International Centre, November 12, 2008.

169. Many have argued that this scenario, however, bodes worse for the United States and other Western countries—a large-scale attack on which would be of far greater symbolic value—than for states such as India. Graham Allison, "Nuclear Terrorism: How Serious a Threat to Russia?", *Russia in Global Affairs*, September/October 2004; Joseph Cirincione, "A Global Assessment of Nuclear Proliferation Threats", Weapons of Mass Destruction Commission, June 2004, available at http://www.wmdcommission.org/files/No10.pdf, accessed March 13, 2009; Proceeds from "Preventing Nuclear Terrorism," conference organised by the Centre for Strategic and International Studies, April 1, 2005.
170. Bharat Karnad, *India's Nuclear Policy*, (Pentagon Press-Praeger Security International, 2008). On the other end of the spectrum, Praful Bidwai and Achin Vanaik argue that nuclear weapons—and in particular the 1998 nuclearisation of India and Pakistan—have heightened Indian, regional, and global insecurity by (a) transforming Kashmir into a potential nuclear flashpoint; (b) diverting government spending from already impoverished populations; and (c) fueling conventional and perhaps even nuclear arms races throughout South Asia, the Middle East, and elsewhere. Praful Bidwai and Achin Vanaik, *New Nukes: India, Pakistan, and Global Nuclear Disarmament* (Signal Books, 2000).
171. Annual Report 2001-2002, Ministry of Defence, Government of India, 2002.
172. Tellis, 2001, op. cit., ch. 2.
173. The report continues, "Even if the United States were to divest itself of its nuclear arsenal, other nations would be unlikely to follow suit. To the contrary, some states would gain incentives to retain or acquire nuclear weapons against a conventionally superior but nuclear-free United States. If nuclear weapons were somehow eliminated, a serious deterioration of the international environment could engender strong incentives for nuclear rearmament. A rapid and competitive race to rebuild nuclear arsenals could increase prospects for a devastating war." Robert Joseph and Ronald Lehman, "US Nuclear Policy in the 21st Century", *Strategic Forum*, NDU Press, Number 145, August 1998, available at http://www.ndu.edu/inss/strforum/SF145/forum145.html, accessed December 29, 2008.
174. General (Retd.) Ved P. Malik, "Seizing the Moment: Highest Priority Steps for 2009", Presentation at the Conference on Breakthrough Measures to Build a New East-West Consensus on Weapons of Mass Destruction and Disarmament, East-West Institute, November 2008.
175. This is in many ways counter to 'conventional' Cold War nuclear doctrines espoused by the United States and erstwhile Soviet Union. "India's refusal to treat nuclear weapons as military tools for uses other than political deterrence is rooted in three

issues. The first such issue is the longstanding tradition of idealist and liberal thought....The second issue is related to the country's traditional organization of civil-military relations. India has one of the most rigid and ironclad systems for ensuring *absolute* civilian control over the military. All decisions pertaining to the nuclear weapons program have been made solely...by India's prime ministers... The third and final issue relates to the desire of Indian security managers to avoid the high costs involved in developing a large and costly nuclear inventory and in redesigning and reequipping conventional forces for the nuclear battlefield." Ashley Tellis, "India's Emerging Nuclear Doctrine: Exemplifying the Lessons of the Nuclear Revolution", *The National Bureau of Asian Research*, Vol. 12, No. 2, May 2001, p. viii. Tellis argues that this is the near unanimous consensus amongst Indian strategic thinkers: "Even India's hawks are usually agreed on this issue: that nuclear deterrence ought not to be treated as a problem that lends itself to solutions based on defense, as the United States did during the Cold War."

176. Perkovich, 2001, op. cit.
177. See, for example, The State Council Information Office of the People's Republic of China, *China's National Defence in 2006*, Beijing, December 2006, available at http://www.chinadaily.com.cn/china/2006-12/29/content_771191.htm.
178. Tellis, 2001, op. cit., p. 73; K Subrahmanyam, "India's Security: The North and North-east Dimension", *Conflict Studies*, Vol. 215, Centre for Security and Conflict Studies, pp. 18-22.
179. Though slightly exaggerated, concerns over the nuclearisation of Arunachal Pradesh itself exist. As Rajeswari Pillai Rajagopalan has written, "Analysts continue to doubt China's NFU pledge, particularly its applicability on its own soil. For instance, how China would respond to a foreign invasion or a war in Tibet or Taiwan is unclear. It will be equally critical to see how China looks at Arunachal Pradesh and whether the NFU applies to Arunachal Pradesh or not. In the not too distant past, Chinese authorities denied visas to officials from Arunachal, reasoning that Arunachal is part of China and, hence, no visas are required...Therefore, it raises concerns as to how China interprets its NFU policy vis-à-vis Arunachal since it considers Arunachal to be its territory." Rajeswari Pillai Rajagopalan, *Chinese Military Strategy* (Observer Research Foundation, Forthcoming), ch. V. It is highly unlikely, however, that either principle would risk nuclear confrontation over Arunachal Pradesh given the relatively low stakes of the region and the high stakes of nuclearisation.
180. Many have argued, however, that there is a scope for "limited conventional warfare" under the nuclear umbrella. See, for example, C. Raja Mohan, "Fernandes Unveils 'Limited War' Doctrine", *The Hindu*, January 25, 2000; See General V. P. Malik's "Limited War and Escalation Control, I and II," New Delhi: Institute of Peace and

Conflict Studies, Article Nos. 1570 and 1571, November 25, 2004; V.R. Raghavan, "Limited War and Nuclear Escalation in South Asia", *The Nonproliferation Review*, Fall-Winter, 2001. The long-term political, economic consequences of even a limited conventional war with Pakistan, however—particular the heightening of anti-India nationalism within Pakistan—are another central deterrent to such conflict. See, for example Neil Padukone, "India's September 12th", Observer Research Foundation (Analysis), December 10, 2008; Zeeshan Haider, Faisal Aziz, Robert Birsel, "Scenarios: What War with India Could Mean for Pakistan", Reuters, December 27, 2008; Ilmas Futehally and Semu Bhatt, "Cost of Conflict between India and Pakistan", Strategic Foresight Group, 2004.

181. Air Marshal M. Asghar Khan, a former Pakistani Air Force Chief, for example, writes that if Pakistan, "a smaller military power…in desperation [used] nuclear weapons in its defense…Pakistan would, as a result, be mortally wounded whereas India would be damaged to a much lesser extent and would still survive as a nation," M. Asghar Khan, "The Nuclear Option", *Dawn* (Karachi), November 2, 2003.
182. This scenario includes the prospect of an Islamist extremist regime, undeterred by nuclear retaliation, seizing control of Pakistan's nuclear arsenal.
183. Tellis, 2001, op. cit.
184. K. Subrahmanyam, *Shedding Shibboleths: India's Evolving Strategic Outlook* (Wordsmiths Press, 2005), p. 145.
185. According to a report by the Natural Resources Defence Council, "an unnamed Defence Ministry source told *Defense News* in late 2004 that in the next five to seven years India will have 300–400 nuclear and thermonuclear weapons distributed to air, sea, and land forces," Robert S. Norris and Hans M. Kristensen, "India's Nuclear Forces 2005", Nuclear Notebook, National Resources Defense Council and the Bulletin of Atomic Scientists, September/October 2005.
186. Ashley J. Tellis, "Toward a 'Force-in-Being': The Logic, Structure, and Utility of India's Emerging Nuclear Posture", in Sumit Ganguly (ed), *India as an Emerging Power* (Routledge Press, 2003), p. 76.
187. Bharath Gopalaswamy, "Missile Defense in India", *Bulletin of the Atomic Scientists*, February 27, 2009.
188. Remarks by former President of India, A. P. J. Abdul Kalam, at the National Seminar on Aerospace Technologies (N-SAT), India Strategic, IDSA Conference Hall, Thursday, September 25, 2008.
189. Remarks by Air Vice Marshal D.C. Kumaria, Assistant Chief of Air Staff Operations (Space), at the National Seminar on Aerospace Technologies (N-SAT), India Strategic, IDSA Conference Hall, Thursday, September 25, 2008.
190. Banerjee, 2008, op. cit.

191. Revolution in Military Affairs (RMA) is a proposition about the future of warfare, related to technological and organisational changes in military structures. RMA had its impetus in American strategic thinking, but is increasingly extending to others as well. It is specifically tied to modern information, communications, and space technologies. See, for example, Thierry Gongora and Harald von Riekhoff (eds), *Toward a Revolution in Military Affairs?: Defense and Security at the Dawn of the Twenty-First Century* (Greenwood Press, 2000).

192. Banerjee, 2008, op. cit., p. 124.

193. Dipankar Banerjee, "Indian Perspectives on Regional Space Security", in John Logsdon and James Clay Moltz (eds), *Collective Security in Space: Asian Perspectives* (George Washington University Space Policy Institute, January 2008).

194. John M. Logsdon and Audrey M. Schaffer (eds), *Perspectives on Space Security* (Space Policy Institute, Elliott School of International Affairs, The George Washington University, December 2005), available at http://www.gwu.edu/~spi/PERSPECTIVES_ON_SPACE_SECURITY.pdf, accessed December 12, 2008.

195. ISRO Founder Vikram Sarabhai attempts to reconcile the ostensible paradox between India's development of an expensive space program and its existence as a developing country, by stating, "There are some who question the relevance of space activities in a developing nation. To us, there is no ambiguity of purpose. We do not have the fantasy of competing with the economically advanced nations in the exploration of the moon or the planets or manned space-flight. But we are convinced that if we are to play a meaningful role nationally, and in the community of nations, we must be second to none in the application of advanced technologies to the real problems of man and society." T.V. Jayan, "Forty Years in Space," *Dream 2047: Monthly Newsletter of Vigyan Prasar,* Vol. 4, March 2002, available at http://www.vigyanprasar.gov.in/dream/mar2002/english.pdf, accessed January 16, 2009.

196. "Chandrayaan-I Successfully put into Earth's Orbit", *Indian Express*, October 22, 2008.

197. Remarks by former President of India A. P. J. Abdul Kalam, at National Seminar on Aerospace Technologies (N-SAT), India Strategic, IDSA Conference Hall, Thursday, September 25, 2008.

198. Lee S. Mason, "A Solar Dynamic Power Option for Space Solar Power", Paper prepared for the 34th Intersociety Energy Conversion Engineering Conference, Vancouver, British Columbia, Canada, August 1–5, 1999, National Aeronautics and Space Administration, Glenn Research Centre, July 1999, available at http://gltrs.grc.nasa.gov/reports/1999/TM-1999-209380.pdf, accessed January 15, 2009.

199. George Friedman, *The Next 100 Years: A Forecast for the 21st Century* (Double Day Press, 2009).
200. John M. Logsdon, James Clay Moltz, Emma S. Hinds (eds), *Collective Security in Space: European Perspectives* (Space Policy Institute, George Washington University, January 2007), available at http://www.gwu.edu/~spi/Collective%20Security%20in%20Space%20-%20European%20Perspectives.pdf, accessed January 21, 2009. See also Lt. Col. Scott Maethner, "Achilles' Heal: Space and Information Power in the 21st Century", Schriever Air Base, *High Frontier*, August 2007. Whether future technologies will be able to minimise the susceptibility of space-based infrastructure to these vulnerabilities remains unseen.
201. John Garstka and David S. Alberts, "Network-Centric Operations Conceptual Framework Version 2.0.", Vienna, VA: Evidenced Based Research, 2004; emphasis added.
202. Brigadier Gurmeet Kanwal, remarks at the National Seminar on Aerospace Technologies (N-SAT), India Strategic, IDSA Conference Hall, Thursday, September 25, 2008.
203. Personal conversation with Assistant Chief of Naval Staff (Air), Rear Admiral V. Shankar, Thursday, September 25, 2008.
204. Gompert, Lachow, and Perkins, 2006, op. cit.
205. George Friedman and Meredith Friedman, *The Future of War: Power, Technology and American World Dominance in the Twenty-First Century* (St. Martin's Griffin Press, 1998).
206. Such forces include sub-national adversaries, many of whose mastery of networking has surpassed that of state militaries and security forces; For such a comparison, see, for example, Yaneer Bar-Yam, *Making Things Work: Solving Complex Problems in a Complex World* (Knowledge Press, 2004), ch. 5 and 9; and Gompert, Lachow, and Perkins, 2006, op. cit., pp. 49-53.
207. David C. Gompert, Irving Lachow, and Justin Perkins, "Battlewise: Gaining Advantage in Networked Warfare", Centre for Technology and National Security Policy, National Defense University, June 2005, available at http://www.ndu.edu/CTNSP/Def_Tech/DTP8%20Battlewise.pdf, accessed January 12, 2009.
208. See, for cxample, George Tanham, "Indian Strategic Thought: An Interpretive Essay", RAND Corporation, 1992, who argues that India's geography and culture, the framing of India's history as a collective, national narrative, and the legacy of the British Raj have resulted in a deficit in Indian strategic thinking. "The inherent pessimism and passivism of the cyclical view [of life] suggests little likelihood of major improvement in life…," a philosophy that restricts the possibility of proactivity to change the status quo, and even of planning for a future that is viewed as unpredictable. Others, however, argue that India has long

had a powerful strategic culture defined by the very founders of the republic. The founders anticipated India's ultimate rise as a global power, and defined a long-term strategic policy accordingly. This policy was inextricably linked to domestic policy such as a strong industrial and economic base, a civilian and military scientific and technological capacity that is driven by a robust educational infrastructure, and concomitant, strong soft-power capacity. See, for example, the revisionist history of Bharat Karnad, *Nuclear Weapons and Indian Security: The Realist Foundations of Strategy* (Macmillan India Ltd., 2005), who argues that despite Nehru's rhetoric focussing on idealism and non-alignment, his initial moves clearly established India under the nuclear umbrella of the West, enabling India to focus on more immediate concerns. Karnad nonetheless argues that this realism was lost with Nehru's death.

209. General Ved. P. Malik (Retd), "Forward", in Gurmeet Kanwal, *Indian Army: Vision 2020* (Harper Collins Publishers, 2008), pp. X
210. Bharat Karnad, "India's Future Plans and Defense Requirements," in N.S. Sisodia and C. Uday Bhaskar (eds)., *Emerging India: Security and Foreign Policy Perspectives* (Institute for Defence Studies and Analyses, published by Bibliophile South Asia, 2005), p. 65.
211. George Tanham, *Indian Strategic Thought: An Interpretive Essay* (RAND Corporation, 1992), p. vii; also addressed in Subrahmanyam, 2005, op. cit.
212. George Tanham, "Indian Strategic Culture", *The Washington Quarterly*, Vol. 15, No. 1, Winter 1992.
213. As Tanham has written, for example, "As long as India sees Pakistan as a threat to its primacy in the subcontinent, and as long as the Pakistanis refuse to accept Indian primacy, tensions will remain, exacerbated by such situations as Kashmir." Tanham, Ibid.
214. Remarks by K. Subrahmanyam, Panel Discussion and Book Release of "India's Nuclear Policy" by Bharat Karnad, India International Centre, November 12, 2008.
215. This idea was further discussed at a panel on "India and the U.S: What Lies Ahead," presented by Ambassador Teresita Schaeffer, Observer Research Foundation, January 30, 2009.
216. Charlie Edwards, *The Case for a National Security Strategy* (Demos UK, February 2007), available at http://www.demos.co.uk/files/Demos_report_the_case_for_a_national_security_strategy.pdf, accessed November 22, 2008; The referenced report focusses on challenges faced by, and solutions prescribed for, the British government, but the common theme of complexity defines the security challenges that both the UK and India face, as well as necessarily proactive solutions thereto.

Micro-Macro Interactions

217. The 'multi-centric' system refers to that of individuals, groups, corporations, and those entities that cannot be classified as 'nation-states.'
218. Other 'macro' structures include, for example, the physical environment, geography and resources, etc.
219. In sociology, this is often referred to as the "agent-structure" problem. See, for example, Anthony Giddens, *The Constitution of Society: Outline of the Theory of Structuration* (Cambridge, Mass: Polity Press, 1984).
220. Togzhan Kassenova, "Central Asia: Regional Security and WMD Proliferation Threats", United Nations Institute for Disarmament Research, *Disarmament Forum*, Vol. 4, 2007, available at http://www.unidir.ch/pdf/articles/pdf-art2684.pdf, accessed January 8, 2009.
221. See, for example, Matthew Bunn, Oleg Bukharin, and Kenneth N. Luongo, *Renewing the Partnership: Recommendations for Accelerated Action to Secure Nuclear Material in the Former Soviet Union* (Princeton, N.J.: Russian-American Nuclear Security Advisory Council, 2000).
222. Kassenova, 2007, op. cit.
223. In January 2006, for example, Georgian authorities interdicted a smuggled shipment of four ounces of enriched uranium destined for "a buyer who…would pay [the smuggler] $1 million and deliver the material to a Muslim man from 'a serious organization,' the authorities say," Lawrence Scott Sheets and William Broad, "Smuggler's Plot Highlights Fear Over Uranium, *New York Times,* January 25, 2007.
224. Bill Powell, Tim McGirk, Ghulam Hasnain, Sayed Talat Hussain, Timothy J. Burger, Elaine Shannon, Scott MacLeod, Andrew Purvis, Simon Robinson, Nahid Siamdoust, "The Man Who Sold the Bomb," *Time Magazine*, Vol. 165, Issue 7, February 14, 2005.
225. Gary Milhollin and Kelly Motz, "Nukes 'R' Us," *New York Times*, March 4, 2004, p. A31.
226. The extent of this network is unknown because (a) A.Q. Khan has been exempt from international interrogation; and (b) the materials that had their source in Khan's network may have extended to areas beyond the control or knowledge of Khan's own operations.
227. 'Irrational' refers to those actors to whom the threat of nuclear retaliation if not a deterrent for initial use.
228. RDDs disperse radioactive material (namely enriched uranium) across a large civilian area using conventional explosives.
229. According to a report by *The Telegraph-India*, in 2003, Bangladeshi authorities detected the theft of semi-processed, "explosive grade" uranium in Bangladesh by

"Islamic fundamentalists groups that [play host] for the al-Qaeda terror network" in that country. Probir Pramanik, "Al-Qaeda Link in Uranium Haul near Balurghat", *The Telegraph India*, June 17, 2003.

230. This government body has controlled all nuclear material, research, and development, with minimal involvement of private sector firms, given the security concerns related to nuclear technology; personal interview with Dr. Suresh Kati, former Managing Director of the Nuclear Power Corporation, December 30, 2008.
231. This contingency is particularly important in the light of the liability debates between India and supplier countries, namely the United States; such clauses would protect supplier firms from legal liability in the case of an accident or attack.
232. See, for example, Ramtanu Maitra, "Prospects Brighten for Kunming Initiative", *Asia Times*, February 12, 2003.
233. John Pomfret, "Tunnel Found on Mexican Border", *Washington Post*, January 27, 2006.
234. "Palestinian Security Uncovers Two Underground Tunnels Along Gaza-Egypt Border", *International Herald Tribune*, September 26, 2006.
235. Ashok Pahalwan, "India Considers Army Tunnel Network for Kashmir Border", Reuters Press, November 3, 2008.
236. Gal Luft and Anne Korin, "Terrorism Goes to Sea", *Foreign Affairs*, November/December 2004.
237. See, for example, Anthony Smith, "State and Sovereignty: Is the State in Retreat?", *New Zealand International Review*, November 1, 1997.
238. P.V. Indiresan, "The Kunming Initiative", *Frontline*, Vol. 17, No. 7, Apr 01-14, 2000.
239. Gabriel Weimann, "Cyberterrorism: How Real is the Threat?", United States Institute of Peace, Special Report No. 119, USIP, December 2004.
240. John Arquilla and David Ronfeldt, "Cyberwar is Coming!" *Comparative Strategy*, Vol. 12, No. 2, Spring 1993, pp. 141–165.
241. Ravi Visvesvaraya Prasad, "Hack the Hackers", *Hindustan Times*, December 19, 2000.
242. Quoted in Robert Marquand and Ben Arnoldy, "China Emerges as Leader in Cyberwarfare", *Christian Science Monitor*, September 14, 2007.
243. Ibid.
244. Visvesvaraya Prasad, 2000, op. cit.
245. Marquand and Arnoldy, 2007, op. cit.
246. See, for example, work by Thomas Friedman, a major proponent of this argument: *The Lexus and the Olive Tree* (New York: Farrar, 1999); and Thomas Friedman, *The World is Flat: A Brief History of the 21st Century* (Farrar, Straus and Giroux, 2005).

247. Lt. Commander Prashant Bakshi, "Security Implications for a Wired India: Challenges Ahead", *Strategic Analysis*, IDSA, Vol. 25, No. 1, April 2001.
248. This section is based on the proceedings of two conferences on Converging Technologies published in William S. Bainbridge and Mihail C. Roco (eds), *Managing Nano-Bio-Info-Cogno Innovations: Converging Technologies in Society* (Springer Press, 2005); and Mihail C. Roco and William S. Bainbridge (eds), *Converging Technologies for Improving Human Performance: Nanotechnology, Biotechnology, Information Technology, and Cognitive Science*, NSF/DOC-Sponsored Report, June 2002.
249. Roco and Bainbridge, Ibid.
250. This would pave the way for enhanced human-computer interface, in which man and machine become united. See, for example, Ray Kurzweil, *The Singularity is Near: When Humans Transcend Biology* (Viking Press, 2005).
251. From the proceeds of a December 2001 workshop on Convergent Technologies to Improve Human Performance in Roco and Bainbridge, 2002, op. cit.
252. Francis Fukuyama, *Our Posthuman Future: Consequences of the Biotechnology Revolution* (New York: Farrar, Strauss, Giroux, 2002).
253. Nicholas Bostrom, "The Transhumanist FAQ: A General Introduction", Version 2.1, World Transhumanist Association, 2003, available at http://transhumanism.org/resources/FAQv21.pdf, accessed January 12, 2009.
254. Bruce Tonn, "Coevolution of Social Science and Emerging Technologies," in William S. Bainbridge and Mihail C. Roco (eds), *Managing Nano-Bio-Info-Cogno Innovations: Converging Technologies in Society* (Springer Press, 2005).
255. James Hughes, "Human Enhancement and the Emergent Technopolitics of the 21st Century," chapter 18 in Roco and Bainbridge, 2005, Ibid., p. 286.
256. Vandana Shiva, *The Violence of the Green Revolution: Ecological Degradation and Political Conflict* (Zed Books, 1992).
257. See, for example, Jack Kalpakian, *Identity, Conflict and Cooperation in International River Systems* (Ashgate Publishing, 2004), chapter 5; and Waslekar, 2005, op. cit.
258. See, for example, the Intergovernmental Panel on Climate Change Fourth Assessment Reports of 2007: Climate Change 2007 - The Physical Science Basis, Contribution of Working Group I to the Fourth Assessment Report of the IPCC; Climate Change 2007 - Impacts, Adaptation and Vulnerability, Contribution of Working Group II to the Fourth Assessment Report of the IPCC; Climate Change 2007 - Mitigation of Climate Change, Contribution of Working Group III to the Fourth Assessment Report of the IPCC
259. This statistic is attributed to a 2008 World Bank Report cited in "One-Third of World's Poor in India: Survey," *Times of India*, August 27, 2008.

260. See, for example, Roger Harrabin, "Climate Change 'Harms World Poor'", BBC, March 24, 2006; and Department for International Development, "Working Internationally to Tackle Climate Change: Managing Climate Change", July 2006.

261. Ashok B. Sharma, "Climate Change to Impact Indian Agriculture: IARI", *The Financial Express*, January 28, 2008.

262. "Past sea level has varied by 10–20 metres for each 1°C change in the global average temperature. The IPCC business-as-usual forecast for 3°C would translate to 20–50 meters of sea level rise." David Archer, *The Long Thaw: How Humans Are Changing the Next 100,000 Years of Earth's Climate* (Princeton University Press, 2008).

263. Andrew Revkin, "Maldives Considers Buying Dry Land if Seas Rise", *New York Times*, November 10, 2008.

264. Cited in Brahma Chellaney, "Climate Change and Security in Southern Asia: Understanding the National Security Implications," *RUSI Journal*, Vol. 152, No. 2, April 2007, p. 62.

265. As one Mumbai slum resident articulated, "We North Indians are not allowed to draw water from these taps. These people claim that the water is meant only for Maharashtrians," Sandeep K.M., "Burning Issue: Water Dispute Divides a Navi Mumbai Slum," *Indian Express*, December 17, 1998.

266. Brahma Chellaney and Heela Najibullah, *On the Frontline of Climate Change: International Security Implications* (Konrad Adenauer Foundation, 2007).

267. The Indus Waters Treaty of 1960 between the Governments of India and Pakistan, available at http://siteresources.worldbank.org/INTSOUTHASIA/Resources/223497-1105737253588/IndusWatersTreaty1960.pdf, accessed December 15, 2008.

268. John Reid, "Water Wars: Climate Change may Spark Conflict", *The Independent*, February 28, 2006.

269. According to S. Padmanabhan, Executive Director (Operations) of Tata Power, Chinese damming of the Brahmaputra "will put almost 40 per cent of India's hydel potential in trouble. India has hydro potential of 1,50,000 MW, of which 50,000 MW is in the North-East. Arunachal Pradesh, mainly fed by Brahmaputra's tributaries — Siang, Subansiri and Lohit — supports development of 28,500 MW hydro projects." S. Padmanabhan, "China, the Brahmaputra and India," *The Hindu Business Line*, April 14, 2009.

270. Neil Pelkey, *The Cauvery Water War* (University of California, Division of Environmental Studies).

271. Amended from http://www.mapsofindia.com/top-ten/geography/india-rivers.gif, Compare Infobase Limited, Copyright 1999, Mapsofindia.com

272. The economic implications of climate change have not been discussed in this review in the interests of brevity. For India, in particular, however, they are vast and profound. For an in-depth view of the economic consequences of climate change, please see Nicholas Stern, "Stern Review on the Economics of Climate Change: Final Report", New Economics Foundation, October 30, 2006.
273. See, for example, The Whitehouse Press Release: *President Bush Discusses Global Climate Change*, June 11, 2001, available at http://www.whitehouse.gov/news/releases/2001/06/20010611-2.html, accessed December 20, 2008.
274. Lavanya Rajamani, "India's Negotiating Position on Climate Change: Legitimate but not Sagacious," Centre for Policy Research, *CPR Issue Brief*, No. 2, 2007.
275. A. Agarwal and Sunita Narain, "Global Warming in an Unequal World: A Case of Environmental Colonialism", Centre for Science and Environment, New Delhi, India, 1991.
276. Anthony Costello, Mustafa Abbas, et al., "Managing the Health Effects of Climate Change: Lancet and University College London Institute for Global Health Commission," *The Lancet,* Vol. 373, No. 9676, pp. 1703, 2009.
277. Rajamani, 2007, op. cit.
278. Costello, Abbas, et al., 2009, op. cit., pp. 1703.
279. O. Dun, F. Gemenne, and R. Stojanov, "Environmentally Displaced Persons: Working Definitions for the EACH-FOR Project," Paper presented at the International Conference on Migration and Development in Ostrava, Czech Republic on September 5, 2007.
280. Dean Nelson, "India Fences off Bangladesh to Keep out Muslim Terror", *Times UK*, November 13, 2005.
281. See, for example, Sundeep Waslekar et al, *The Final Settlement: Restructuring India-Pakistan Relations* (The Strategic Foresight Group, 2005).
282. Aashti Salman, "India Moves First on Kishanganga Project," ORF Analysis, January 6, 2009.
283. "International Energy Outlook: 2009," Energy Information Administration, United States Department of Energy, May 2009, p. 13.
284. World Energy Outlook: Part III - The Role of Energy in Climate Policy," International Energy Agency, OECD Publishing, November 28, 2008, p. 390.
285. The issue of inequitable development patterns that encourage urbanisation will be discussed at length in the next section on "Economics in the Realm of Security," namely the sub-section on "Urbanization, Migration and Development."
286. Suneet Weling, "Why India Needs a Sovereign Wealth Fund", Rediff News, December 29, 2007.
287. Flynt Leverett, "Black is the New Green", *The National Interest*, January/February 2008.

288. "When Trade Winds Smell Sweet", *The Economist*, April 10, 2008; "Opportunities for Constructing Win-Win Situations by Reconciling Business Profitability with Broader Social Objectives in External Engagement", Panel at International Conference: Engaging with a Resurgent Africa, Conference hosted by the Observer Research Foundation and the Rose Luxembourg Foundation, November 20-21, 2008.
289. "When Trade Winds Smell Sweet", *The Economist*, April 10, 2008; "There be Dragons", *The Economist*, November 6, 2008.
290. John Perkins, *Confessions of an Economic Hitman* (Berrett-Koehler Publishers, 2004); William Easterly, *The White Man's Burden: Why the West's Efforts to Aid the Rest Have Done So Much Ill and So Little Good* (Penguin Press, 2006).
291. Matthew T. Simpson, "Mitigating Volatility: Protecting Chinese Investments in Post-Conflict Regions", *Journal of World Investment and Trade,* Vol. 9, June 2008, p. 317; "There be Dragons", *The Economist*, November 6, 2008.
292. Ajai Sahni, "Survey of Conflicts and Resolution in India's Northeast", *Faultlines: Writings on Conflict & Resolution*, Vol 12, 2002, South Asia Terrorism Portal and Institute for Conflict Management, available at http://www.satp.org/satporgtp/publication/faultlines/volume12/Article3.htm, accessed May 12, 2009.
293. This phenomenon has also been referred to as a "Gross Terror-Economy Product" by sources such as the Strategic Foresight Group. See, for example, Sundeep Waslekar et al., "Cost of Conflict Between India and Pakistan", Strategic Foresight Group, 2004, available at http://www.strategicforesight.com/costofconflict.htm, accessed January 12, 2009.
294. Atul Aneja, "CVC Told to Probe Major Defence Deals", *The Hindu*, February 6, 2000; Lok Sabha Secretariat, Standing Committee on Defence: Ministry of Defence Demands for Grants, Thirteenth Lok Sabha, 2001, available at http://164.100.24.208/ls/committeeR/Defence/11.pdf, accessed February 12, 2009.
295. James A. Huston, "The Military Industrial Complex," in Alexander DeConde, Richard Dean Burns, and Fredrik Logevall (eds), *Encyclopedia of American Foreign Policy* (Simon and Shuster, 2002).
296. Indeed, it has long been stated that the United States' military spending exceeds the combined total of the rest of the world. Per capita, the United States and Israel spend \$1604 and \$1430, respectively, while China and India spend \$31.2 and \$18.5, respectively. Petter Stålenheim, Damien Fruchart, Wuyi Omitoogun and Catalina Perdomo, "Military Expenditure", *SIPRI Yearbook 2006: Armaments, Disarmament and International Security* (The Stockholm International Peace Research Institute, Oxford University Press, June 2006), ch. 8. This is certainly contingent not only on the MIC, but each countries' perceived strategic concerns:

the United States as the sole superpower and global hegemon, coming from a history of a Cold War with the Soviet Union; and Israel as a state surrounded by hostile neighbours with whom it has a history of violent confrontation.

297. For example, the B2 bomber has a component that is produced in every single state in the United States; no elected official would call for the termination of its production, fearing electoral losses. Eugene Jarecki, "Why We Fight", Sony Studios, 2006.
298. This expansion will be discussed further in the next section, "Conclusion: Managing Security in a Complex Age."
299. The US has also experienced what Noriel Roubini and Brad Setser have termed a "Borrower-Industrial Complex" that links government to financial elites, enabling the latter to exert excessive influence on the former. Particularly in the 1990s' "dot-com" and financial booms, a major "realignment of national interest-group influence and the escalating political clout of the financial services industry [took place]. By the 1990s, policy favoritism had become endemic." Thus, the proposed change to even the financial sector may face challenges from similarly vested interests, which, in 1998, for example, "successfully mobilized to repeal the Glass-Steagall Act, the New Deal statute mandating the separation of commercial banking, investment banking, and insurance." See Kevin Phillips, *American Theocracy: The Peril and Politics of Radical Religion, Oil, and Borrowed Money in the 21st Century* (Viking Press, 2006).
300. See, for example, Population Division of the Department of Economic and Social Affairs of the United Nations Secretariat, World Population Prospects: The 2006 Revision and World Urbanization Prospects: The 2007 Revision.
301. According to Hania Zlotnik, Director of Department of Economic and Social Affairs' Population Division of the United Nations, "two scenarios are likely [for India] - either people would migrate to cities such as Mumbai, or one-time rural areas would transition into urban centers by generating other activities as has been happening in China." "Over 55% of India Will Live in Urban Areas by 2050," *Asian Age*, February 28, 2008; See also, "World Urbanization Prospects: The 2007 Revision," United Nations Department of Economic and Social Affairs: Population Division, 2008.
302. Sundeep Waslekar, Ilmas Futehally, Leena Pillai, *Rethinking India's Future: Prosperity of the Periphery* (Strategic Foresight Group, 2002).
303. This is not to endorse a causal relationship between poverty and crime, but rather, to demonstrate that poverty is often an enabling factor for manipulation by criminal elements.
304. "A Specter Haunting India" *The Economist*, August 17, 2006.
305. Harivansh, "Roots and Causes: The Case of Jharkhand," in P.V. Ramana, *The*

Naxal Challenge: Causes, Linkages, and Policy Options (Pearson-Longman Press and ORF, 2008), pp. 18-24.

306. Ajai Sahni, "A Riot of Red Flags," *Himal South Asian*, Kathmandu, Vol. 21 No. 9, September 2008.
307. "A Specter Haunting India", *The Economist,* August 17, 2006.
308. Ambika Pandit, "Homeless, Facing Identity Crisis", *Times of India*, January 25, 2009.
309. This statistic is attributed to a 2008 World Bank Report cited in "One-Third of World's Poor in India: Survey," *Times of India*, August 27, 2008.
310. George Friedman of Stratfor, for example, argues that, "India's problem is that it is not one country. It is a group of countries driven together by the British with a central government but with tremendous power still vested in the states and the state bureaucracies. These states have unique ideologies, some of which are very open to foreign investment and some of which are violently opposed...The bureaucracy is not inefficient. It is set up in various states to limit investment... We do not see the forces inside of India that will change this basic dynamic. So we see that, whereas the Chinese Central Committee in 1975 put in motion a set of national decisions as to what was going to happen, there is no similar central authority in India to do that." George Friedman and Joanne J. Myers, "The Next 100 Years: A Forecast for the 21st Century," Seminar organised by the Carnegie Council, New York City, January 28, 2009, Transcript available at http://www.cceia.org/resources/transcripts/0111.html, accessed February 18, 2009.
311. Achin Vanaik and Paul R. Brass (eds), *Competing Nationalism in South Asia: Essays for Asghar Ali Engineer* (Sangam Books, 2002).
312. James Rosenau, "Governing the Ungovernable: The Challenge of a Global Disaggregation of Authority", Paper prepared for presentation at the annual conference of the International Society for New Institutional Economics, Tucson, Arizona, Sept. 30-Oct 3, 2004.
313. The 'disaggregation of authority' refers to a weakening of territoriality, which has led to a lessening of sovereignty and a reduction in the amount of power held by states. James Rosenau, *Distant Proximities: Dynamics Beyond Globalization* (Princeton: Princeton University Press, 2003).
314. Benedict Anderson, *Imagined Communities* (Verso Press, 1990), ch. 3.
315. Miriam Cooke and Bruce Lawrence (eds), *Muslim Networks from Hajj to Hip Hop: Islamic Civilization and Muslim Networks* (The University of North Carolina Press, 2005).
316. See, for example, Asghar Ali Engineer, *Islamic World and the Crisis of Modernism, Islam and Modern Age* (Mumbai: Institute of Islamic Studies, January 2002);

Sean Yom, "Islam and Globalization: Secularism, Religion, and Radicalism," *Internationale Politik und Gesellschaft*, Vol. 5: No. 4, Autumn 2002, Reprinted in Alfred Pfaller and Marika Lerch (eds), Challenges of Globalization: New Trends in International Politics and Society, (New Brunswick: Transaction, 2005); Khalid Medani, "Globalization, Informal Markets and the Rise of Islamic Extremism: Giving Some Context to the Attacks of 9/11", Paper presented at the annual meeting of the International Studies Association, Le Centre Sheraton Hotel, Montreal, Quebec, Canada, March 17, 2004; Salwa Ismail, "Locating and Dislocating Islamism: Globalization, the City, and Islamist Politics," Paper presented at Cities and Fundamentalisms, a conference organised by the Woodrow Wilson at the University of California at Berkeley, November 30, 2007.

317. The author subscribes to certain tenets of the 'modernist' school of nationalism, and puts 'Pan-Islamism' within a similar framework. However, the phenomenon of nationalist reignition is especially pronounced in Islam due to several other factors as well. First, the rise of 'Pan-Islamic' thought—for purposes of legitimate spirituality, political reform, and violence (the three of which are often interlinked)—is particularly pronounced because the broad geographic dispersion of Muslims around the world makes connectivity amongst the community more vast, indeed 'global,' and long-distance weak ties become more plentiful, instrumental, and meaningful in Islam and Islamism. Second, a 'civilisational void' has permeated much of the Islamic world for the past few centuries. While once leading the world intellectually, culturally, philosophically, economically, politically, and otherwise, the same is not the case today, compelling large-scale crises of knowledge and identity. Through this framework, 'Arab nationalism' can be seen as an initial response to that crisis. But with the failure of pan-Arabism and the wider reach of the internet and the Islamic world itself, pan-Islamism has risen as a response. [See, for example, Bernard Lewis, *What Went Wrong? Western Impact and Middle Eastern Response* (Oxford: Oxford University Press, 2001)]; Sundeep Waslekar, *An Inclusive World: In Which the West, Islam, and the Rest have a Stake* (Strategic Foresight Group, 2007); for a discussion specifically of the spiritual void within the Muslim world in recent centuries, see Seyyed Hossein Nasr, *Islam and the Plight of Modern Man* (Kazi Publications, 2001). Third, the poor quality of governance and management of most Islamic countries in the modern era has similarly driven the rise of Islamism. This is particularly true of many Gulf states, that have vast oil reserves and financial capital, but whose leaders have largely squandered these resources in ways that often feed political, economic and cultural inertia within the Islamic world, weakening any legitimacy of the state, and contributing to the identity-based void. [See, for example, Hossein Askari, *The Middle East Oil Exporters: What Happened to Economic Development*? (Cheltenham, UK:

Edward Elgar Publishing, 2006)].

318. For an analysis of the role of new forms of mass media in solidifying a pro-Hindutva political discourse, see, for example, Arvind Rajagopal, *Politics after Television: Religious Nationalism and the Reshaping of the Indian Public* (Cambridge University Press, 2001).
319. Thomas Blom Hansen, *The Saffron Wave: Democracy and Hindu Nationalism in Modern India* (Oxford: Oxford University Press, 1999), ch. 3-5.
320. This is not to discount the increased level and scale of activism by groups affiliated with the Vishwa Hindu Parishad (VHP), Rashtriya Swayamsevak Sangh, (RSS) and the Bharatiya Janata Party (BJP), which contributed greatly to the rise of the 'Hindutva' movement.
321. Yossi Shain, remarks at "Transnational Linkages of Middle Eastern Diasporas to their Countries of Origin" panel discussion at a conference on Shifting Conceptions of Citizenship in the Middle East, organised by the George Washington University Institute of Middle East Studies, November 12, 2007.
322. 'Tools of globalisation' refers in part to the increasing mobility of persons through cheap transportation and diminished barriers to migration, the rise of information and communications technologies, and the erosion of state boundaries—including a deregulation of financial inflows in India.
323. Perhaps the most prominent exception is Singapore, which has a very small population and geography, and has had an authoritarian government throughout its history to enforce the nation-state building process. Otherwise, the supra-national organisation of the European Union is testing the possibilities of multi-nationality within a common political and institutional framework; but micro-level phenomena have challenged even that cohesion.

Conclusion: Managing Security in a Complex Age

324. Robert Jervis, "Complex Systems: The Role of Interactions," in David Alberts and Thomas Czerwinski (eds), *Complexity, Global Politics, and National Security* (Washington, DC: National Defense University Press, 1996).
325. Gill, 1997, op. cit.
326. Julius Ribeiro, *Bullet for a Bullet: My Life as a Police Officer* (Penguin Books).
327. According to Articles 246(3) and 162 of the Indian Constitution.
328. Vandana Shiva, *The Violence of the Green Revolution: Ecological Degradation and Political Conflict* (Zed Books, 1992).
329. Vandana Shiva, "The Green Revolution in the Punjab," *The Ecologist*, Vol. 21, No. 2, March-April 1991.
330. James Rosenau, "Many Damn Things Simultaneously: Complexity Theory and World Affairs," Paper presented at the Conference on Complexity, Global Politics,

and National Security, sponsored by the National Defense University and the RAND Corporation, Washington, D.C., November 13, 1996.

331. Sadako Ogata and Amartya Sen, Final Report of the Commission on Human Security, Commission on Human Security, May 1, 2003, available at http://www.humansecurity-chs.org/finalreport/English/FinalReport.pdf, accessed January 16, 2009.

332. This conceptualisation was first articulated in "Final Report of the Presidential Transition Office: Classroom Simulation," Project on Forward Engagement, Fall 2007, a project of which the author was a chair.

333. Hans J. Morgenthau, *Politics Among Nations: The Struggle for Power and Peace* (Alfred A. Knopf Press, 1948).

334. The name of this concept, the Red Queen Hypothesis is based on Lewis Carroll's Through the Looking Glass, in which the Red Queen tells Alice, "It takes all the running you can do, to keep in the same place. If you want to get somewhere else, you must run at least twice as fast as that!" Quoted in Francis Heylighen and Donald Campbell, "Selection of Organization at the Social Level: Obstacles and Facilitators of Metasystem Transitions", *World Futures: the Journal of General Evolution,* Vol. 45, 1995, pp. 181-212; See also Leigh Van Valen, "A New Evolutionary Law", *Evolutionary Theory*, Vol. 1, 1973, pp. 1-30.

335. In the United States, for example, the state was long an instrument of oppression against Black American minorities. When the latter began to organise and agitate, both violently and peacefully through democratic institutions, the state continued its oppression, citing security concerns, but ultimately realising that it had been in the wrong. See, for example, Aldon D. Morris, *The Origins of the Civil Rights Movement: Black Communities Organizing for Change* (New York: The Free Press, 1984). The same can be said of Dalit activism against social and state institutions in post-Independence India, or even the Indian Independence Movement in British India.

336. Robert Karniol, "Multi-Arm Path to National Security", *The Straits Times*, October 20, 2008.

337. Yaneer Bar-Yam, *Making Things Work: Solving Complex Problems in a Complex World* (Knowledge Press, 2004).

338. David Gompert, Irving Lachow, and Justin Perkins, *Battle-Wise: Seeking Time-Information Superiority in Networked Warfare* (Centre for Technology and National Security Policy, National Defense University Press, 2006); see also James Surowiecki, *The Wisdom of Crowds: Why the Many are Smarter than the Few and How Collective Wisdom Shapes Business, Economies, Societies, and Nations* (New York: Random House Press, 2004).

339. D. Shyam Babu, "National Security Council: Yet Another Ad Hoc Move?", in

P.R. Kumaraswamy (ed), *Security Beyond Survival: Essays for K. Subrahmanyam* (Sage Publications, 2004).

340. A.G. Noorani, "End this Sham: National Security Council", *The Statesman* (New Delhi), June 16, 1999; K. Subrahmanyam, "Wanted Long-term Defence Planning: Elite Indifferent to National Security", The Tribune (Chandigarh), November 5, 2000.
341. Gompert, Lachow, and Perkins, 2006, op. cit.
342. NSG hubs have since been established at Mumbai, Chennai, Kolkata and Hyderabad, See, for example, Vishwa Mohan, NSG hubs at Mumbai, Chennai, Kolkata, and Hyderabad, *Times of India*, December 22, 2008.
343. See, for example, Omar Khalidi, *Khaki and the Ethnic Violence in India: Army, Police and Paramilitary Forces During Communal Riots* (Three Essays Collective, 2003).
344. Shashi Tharoor, "Muslims and the Indian Police", *Times of India*, December 7, 2008.
345. As a result of long-term engagement with Muslim communities, the NYPD realised that "it was not the regular mosque-goers they had to be concerned about, but rather those who had withdrawn from an immigrant mainstream that didn't approve of their radicalism." While this perhaps seems an obvious assumption, it was vastly divergent from mainstream Western understandings of counter-terrorism and community policing, and was only understood through close-knit interaction and integration with minority communities. Jonathan Mahler, "Cops and Bombers: Book Review of *Security the City: Inside America's Best Counterterror Force-The NYPD,* by Christopher Dickey, Simon & Schuster," *New York Times*, January 30, 2009.
346. Suketu Mehta, "The New Faces of America", *Forbes Magazine*, May 7, 2007.
347. Ralph Stacey, *Strategic Management and Organizational Dynamics* (London, UK: Pitman Publishing, 1996); Ralph Stacey, *Complexity and Creativity in Organizations* (San Francisco: Berrett-Koehler, 1996); Ralph Stacey, *Strategic Management and Organizational Dynamics: The Challenge of Complexity* (London: Financial Times Management, 1999).
348. Howard Eisner, *Managing Complex Systems: Thinking Outside the Box* (Wiley-Interscience, 2005).
349. For the specifics of social network analysis see, for example, Karen Stephenson, *Quantum Theory of Trust* (Pearson Press, 2006); Robert L. Cross and Andrew Parker, *The Hidden Power of Social Networks: Understanding How Work Really Gets Done in Organizations* (Harvard Business School Press, 2004).
350. See, for example, Tony Wakefield, Dave McNally, et al, *Introduction to Mobile Communications: Technology, Services, Markets* (Auerbach Publications, 2007).

351. See, for example, Arquilla and Ronfeldt, 2002, op. cit.
352. Neil Padukone, "India's September 12th," Observer Research Foundation (Analysis), December 10, 2008.